Big Green Egg Cookbook 2021-2020

800-Day Flavorful Succulent Barbecue Recipes for Beginners and Advanced Users | Master the Full Potential of Your Ceramic Grill

Hance Lirous

Table of Contents

Introduction

Big Green Egg Cookbook 2021-2020: delicious recipes and step by step directions to enjoy smoking with ceramic grill. Whether you are a beginner meat smoker or looking to go beyond the basics, the book gives you the tools and tips you need to start that perfectly smoked meat.

"Smoking is an art". With a little time & practice, even you can become an expert. To find one which smoking technique works for you, you must experiment with different woods & cooking methods. Just cook the meat over indirect heat source & cook it for hours. When smoking your meats, it's very important that you let the smoke to escape & move around. With white smoke, you can boost the flavor of your food. In addition to this statement, you can preserve the nutrition present in the food as well.

Big Green Egg Cookbook 2021-2020 is specifically celebrating this versatile ceramic cooker. Available in five sizes, Big Green Egg ceramic cookers can sear, grill, smoke, roast, and bake. Here is the gift egg heads have been waiting for, offering a variety of cooking and baking recipes encompassing the cooker's capabilities as a grill, a smoker, and an oven.

Chapter 1: Cooker That Grills, Bake, And Smoke

The Big Green Egg Cooker is an outdoor cooking unit that lets you cook, grill, bake and smoke the food over a coal-fired heating system. The unit comes with a flip lid, a cooking space to carry the coals, the heat vents, and a temperature gauge to maintain the heat inside. You can place different iron pans, cooking pots, and suitable woks inside the cooker to cook food of your choice.

Why Buy the Big Green Cooker?

Before getting into the details of the Big Green Egg Cooker, it is important to understand all the pros of using a charcoal-fired Big green egg cooker.

- **Convenient Outdoor Cooking**

The Big Green Egg Cooker offers convenient outdoor cooking. The cooker comes with a lid that keeps the environment clean and infuses great flavours in the food. And you can take the cooking unit to any outdoor space and cook. It works well because it does not need any electric supply to function. As long as you have a good supply of charcoal to fill the cooker's pot and a lighter to light it up, you are good to go.

- **Temperature Control and Vents**

The function of the thermo-gauge, a top vent, and the lower vent of the cooker are to maintain the internal temperature of the Big Green Egg Cooker. In other charcoal grills, we cannot maintain it manually because there is no gauge to keep track of the temperature once the fire is made, whereas, in the charcoal-fired Big green egg cooker, the temperature rightly indicates the rising or decreasing temperature us.

- **User-Friendly:**

Since in charcoal-fired Big Green Egg Cooker, you add coal to the bottom, and once it is lit, you can use it for 2-3 sessions; it is much less dangerous than other charcoal grills because you don't have to toss and move around the hot coal to maintain the heat. You can change the temperature and keep track of it using the

- **Easy Cleaning**

The convEGGtor placed inside the egg cooker can be easily removed after every cooking session, and it can be washed afterward. Thus, cleaning becomes much easier for these Big green egg cookers.

- **Sturdy Built**

One of the best features of the charcoal-fired Big Green Egg Cookers is their sturdy exterior and firm built, which makes it safe to use when placed carefully over a stand that stands straight with no imbalance.

Chapter 2: Understanding the Big Green Cooker

The Big Green Egg Works as simple as any other charcoal grill or smoker, but in this cooking unit to get to control the temperature inside the cooking pod using the air circulation. The more the airflow through the pod, the more the flames will be produced, and the temperature will increase. To do so, there are two vents in the cooker:

Vents present at the top of the cooker allow the hot air to release into the air, thus decreasing the temperature. By removing the cover from the vent, the temperature can be decreased.

The vents at the bottom of the cooker comes with a cover; the more the vent is opened, the more the air is flown through the pod, and the temperature is increased.

Thus, the opening and closing of the top and bottom vents control the temperature inside the cooker. The gauge present in front of the lid indicates the temperature inside the cooker. This helps you to keep track of temperature without using any thermometer.

How Does it work?

The following steps must be taken to prepare a newly bought charcoal-fired Big green egg cooker. Clean it using a clean cloth and prepare the device for cooking:

1. First, prepare the device and set over its stand or a nest. The machine must be set on a sturdy base.
2. Now fill the fire pot of the green egg cook with charcoal pieces of medium sizes.
3. Remove the cooker chimney cap and place the adjustable vent on top.
4. Lit the charcoal pieces using an electric or glass lighter.
5. Keep it open until the charcoals start burning and flames settle down.
6. Cover the cooker's lid and keep the vents closed until the desired temperature is reached.
7. To stop the cooker's temperature from rising any further, open the vent on top of the cooker.
8. If the temperature has to be increased, then gradually open the vent at the bottom to increase until the desired temperature is reached.

Cooking Steps:

1. Once your Big Green Egg cooker is all set and preheated, you can add food for cooking.

2. To cook food indirectly in the cooker, you will have to place a convEGGtor, which is like a round tray that covers the grills of the cooker.
3. And to cook directly, do not use the convEGGtor and place food directly on the grilling grates.
4. You can also place a Dutch oven or a wok on the plate to cover the charcoal to turn it into a charcoal stove.
5. Now add the food to the cooker, cover, and cook for the desired cooking time.
6. Keep an eye on the temperature gauge and make use of the vents to keep the temperature in control.
7. Serve your freshly cooked, baked, grilled, or smoked food.

Cleaning and Maintenance

The following important steps will help you clean your cooker after every 2-3 cooking session. It is noteworthy here that cleaning keeps the cooker in better condition. We all know that after every cooking session, a large amount of grease, soot, and ash is left behind. It is important to empty it before refilling it.

- Remember that the longer you will leave the grease on the trays, the hard it will get to wipe it off. You can clean the trays once they are cooled enough to handle without damaging anything.
- To clean the grilling racks, use a pumice stone, wood scraper, or a ball of foil to gently scrape off all the food particles stuck to the grill. Avoid using the stainless-steel wire brush as it damages the ceramic coating on the grills.
- Once the food particles are scraped off, use a wet cloth to wipe off all the grease. Wear gloves to clean the grills grate as they can be sticky after cooking.
- Avoid using any chemical or acidic cleaners as they also damage the ceramic coating of the accessories.
- The next step is to clean the lid and the firepot. The ash present in the firepot can be cleaned using the vacuum cleaner, but you can only vacuum when the cooker is cold, and it is unplugged.
- After 4-5 sessions of cooking, remove the chimney cap a wash it with warm soapy water. Gently wipe or scrape off the soot from the chimney using BBQ wipes or other non-metallic scrubs.
- Now using cleaning wipes or any moist cloth to wipe the cooker from inside and out.
- When the cooker is not in use, keep it over and protected. The cooker must not be exposed to the rain.
- Wipe the temperature gauge gently with a cleaning wipe.
- The food probes can be scrubbed and washed with soapy water to clean them

thoroughly and keep them contamination-free.

Chapter 3: Breakfast Recipes

Breakfast Bake

Serving: 6
Prep Time: 10 minutes
Cooking Time: 50 minutes

Ingredients

- 24 oz bulk pork sausage
- 1 medium bell pepper, chopped
- 1 medium onion, chopped
- 3 cups frozen hash brown potatoes
- 2 cups shredded Cheddar cheese
- 1 cup Bisquick mix
- 2 cups of milk
- ¼ teaspoon pepper
- 4 eggs

Method:

1. Adjust the Big Green Egg cooker temperature to 350 degrees F with convEGGtor.
2. Whisk Bisquick with milk, eggs, and pepper in a mixer.
3. Sauté pork sausage, onion, and bell pepper in a 10-inch skillet over medium heat.
4. Stir cook until the sausage turns brown in color, then transfer to a baking dish.
5. Toss in potatoes, 1 ½ cup cheese, and the Bisquick mixture.
6. Bake the mixture for 45 minutes in the preheated Big Green Egg Cooker
7. Drizzle the remaining cheese over the casserole and bake for 5 minutes.
8. Serve.

Nutritional Information per Serving:

- Calories 322
- Total Fat 11.8 g
- Saturated Fat 2.2 g
- Cholesterol 56 mg
- Sodium 321 mg
- Total Carbs 14.6 g
- Dietary Fiber 4.4 g
- Sugar 8 g
- Protein 17.3 g

Crispy Bacon

Serving: 4
Prep Time: 5 minutes
Cooking Time: 10 minutes

Ingredients:

- 6 bacon slices
- ½ onion, sliced
- 1/4 cup cheddar cheese, grated
- 5 black olives, sliced
- ½ cup avocado mash

Method:

1. Adjust the Big Green Egg cooker temperature to 375 degrees F with convEGGtor.
2. Grease a baking dish with a cooking spray.
3. Arrange the bacon slices in the baking dish.
4. Bake for 10 minutes in the preheated Big Green Egg Cooker until crispy.
5. Top the bacon slices with avocado mash, vegetables, and cheese.
6. Serve.

Nutritional Information per Serving:

- Calories 174
- Total Fat 12.3 g
- Saturated Fat 4.8 g
- Cholesterol 32 mg
- Sodium 597 mg
- Total Carbs 4.5 g
- Fiber 0.6 g
- Sugar 1.9 g
- Protein 12 g

Banana Bread

Serving: 6
Prep Time: 10 minutes
Cooking Time: 25 minutes

Ingredients

- 4 medium bananas, peeled and sliced
- ¼ cup plain Greek yogurt
- 2 large eggs
- 1/2-ounce vanilla extract
- 10 oz. all-purpose flour
- ¾ cup of sugar
- 3 oz. oat flour
- 1 teaspoon baking powder
- 1 teaspoon baking soda
- 3/4 teaspoon kosher salt
- 3/4 teaspoon ground cinnamon
- 1/2 teaspoon ground cloves
- 1/4 teaspoon ground nutmeg
- 3/4 cup coconut oil
- 1 cup toasted pecan

Method:

1. Adjust the Big Green Egg cooker temperature to 350 degrees F with convEGGtor.
2. Layer a 10.5 by 5.5 inches loaf pan with a parchment sheet and keep it aside.
3. Mash the banana in a suitable bowl and add eggs, vanilla, and Greek yogurt, then mix well.
4. Cover this banana yogurt mixture and leave it for 30 minutes.
5. Meanwhile, mix cinnamon, flour, sugar, baking powder, oat flour, salt, baking soda, coconut oil, cloves, and nutmeg in a mixer.
6. Now slowly add banana mash mixture to the flour and continue mixing until smooth.
7. Fold in nuts and mix gently until evenly incorporated.
8. Spread this banana-nut batter in the prepared loaf pan.
9. Bake in the preheated Big Green Egg Cooker for 25 minutes.
10. Slice and serve.

Nutritional Information per Serving:

- Calories 331
- Total Fat 2.5 g
- Saturated Fat 0.5 g
- Cholesterol 35 mg
- Sodium 595 mg
- Total Carbs 69 g
- Fiber 12.2 g
- Sugar 12.5 g
- Protein 8.7g

Pepperoni Omelet

Serving: 6
Prep Time: 5 minutes
Cooking Time: 15 minutes

Ingredients:

- 6 eggs
- 15 pepperoni slices
- 2 tablespoons butter
- 4 tablespoons cream
- Salt, to taste
- Black pepper, to taste

Method:

1. Adjust the Big Green Egg cooker temperature to 350 degrees F with convEGGtor.
2. Mix all of its ingredients in a bowl and pour into a buttered pan.
3. Bake the egg mixture in the preheated Big Green Egg Cooker for 15 minutes.
4. Serve warm.

Nutritional Information per Serving:

- Calories 170
- Total Fat 14.7 g
- Saturated Fat 4.4 g
- Cholesterol 190 mg
- Sodium 346 mg
- Total Carbs 0.6 g
- Fiber 0 g
- Sugar 0.5 g
- Protein 8.8 g

Butter Eggs

Serving: 3
Prep Time: 5 minutes
Cooking Time: 10 minutes

Ingredients:

- 4 eggs
- 1 tablespoon butter
- Salt, to taste
- Black pepper, to taste

Method:

1. Adjust the Big Green Egg cooker temperature to 350 degrees F with convEGGtor.
2. Beat all the buttered egg ingredients in a baking pan.
3. Bake the eggs mixture for 10 minutes in the preheated Big Green Egg Cooker
4. Serve warm with toasts.

Nutritional Information per Serving:

- Calories 118
- Total Fat 9.7 g
- Saturated Fat 4.3 g
- Cholesterol 228 mg
- Sodium 160 mg
- Total Carbs 0.5 g
- Fiber 0 g
- Sugar 0.5 g
- Protein 7.4 g

Raisin Muffins

Serving: 6
Prep Time: 10 minutes
Cooking Time: 22 minutes

Ingredients

- 1 cup wheat bran
- 1 cup boiling water
- 4 oz. plain, non-fat Greek yogurt
- 2 large eggs
- 1 ½ cup whole wheat flour
- 5 1/2 oz. all-purpose flour
- ¾ cup of sugar
- ½ ounce ground cinnamon
- 2 teaspoons baking powder
- 3/4 teaspoon kosher salt
- 1/4 teaspoon baking soda
- 1/8 teaspoon grated nutmeg
- 6 oz. butter
- 1 cup golden raisins
- 3/4-ounce flaxseed

Method:

1. Adjust the Big Green Egg cooker temperature to 400 degrees F with convEGGtor.
2. Mix wheat bran with boiling water in a bowl and leave it for 5 minutes.
3. Add eggs, wheat flour, sugar, Greek yogurt, cinnamon, salt, baking soda, baking powder, butter, and nutmeg into the wheat bran, then mix well in a mixer.
4. Stir in raisins and mix the batter gently.
5. Divide this bran muffin batter into 12 greased muffin cups.
6. Bake in the preheated Big Green Egg Cooker for 18 minutes.
7. Serve fresh.

Nutritional Information per Serving:

- Calories 212
- Total Fat 11.8 g
- Saturated Fat 2.2 g
- Cholesterol 23mg
- Sodium 321 mg
- Total Carbs 14.6 g
- Dietary Fiber 4.4 g
- Sugar 8 g
- Protein 17.3 g

Ham Spinach

Serving: 4
Prep Time: 5 minutes
Cooking Time: 25 minutes

Ingredients:

- 14-ounces ham, sliced
- 8 teaspoons cream
- 2 tablespoons unsalted butter, melted
- 1½ pounds fresh baby spinach
- Salt to taste
- Black pepper, to taste

Method:

1. Adjust the Big Green Egg cooker temperature to 360 degrees F with convEGGtor.
2. Melt butter in a pan and add spinach to cook for 3 minutes.
3. Butter 4 ramekins and add ham slice to each ramekin.
4. Top the ham with spinach and cream in each ramekin.
5. Sprinkle salt and pepper on top.
6. Bake then for 25 minutes in the preheated Big Green Egg Cooker.
7. Serve warm.

Nutritional Information per Serving:

- Calories 171
- Total Fat 10.3 g
- Saturated Fat 4.6 g
- Cholesterol 49 mg
- Sodium 1008 mg
- Total Carbs 6.8 g
- Fiber 3.4 g
- Sugar 0.6 g
- Protein 14.3 g

Onion Tofu Scramble

Serving: 4
Prep Time: 5 minutes
Cooking Time: 20 minutes

Ingredients:

- 1 block tofu, pressed and cubed into 1-inch pieces
- 1 medium onion, sliced
- 1 tablespoon butter
- ½ cup cheddar cheese, grated
- Salt to taste,
- Black pepper, to taste

Method:

1. Adjust the Big Green Egg cooker temperature to 350 degrees F with convEGGtor.
2. Season the diced tofu with salt and black pepper in a bowl.
3. Add all the ingredients to a buttered baking pan.
4. Bake the tofu mixture in the preheated Big Green Egg Cooker for 20 minutes.
5. Enjoy with warm bread.

Nutritional Information per Serving:

- Calories 109
- Total Fat 8.5 g
- Saturated Fat 5 g
- Cholesterol 22 mg
- Sodium 112 mg
- Total Carbs 3.2 g
- Fiber 0.8 g
- Sugar 1.4 g
- Protein 5.7 g

Blueberry-Lemon Scones

Serving: 6
Prep Time: 10 minutes
Cooking Time: 25 minutes

Ingredients

- 2 cups all-purpose flour
- 1 tablespoon baking powder
- 2 teaspoons sugar
- 1 teaspoon kosher salt
- 2 oz. of refined coconut oil
- 1 cup fresh blueberries
- ¼ ounce lemon zest
- 8 oz. of coconut milk

Method:

1. Adjust the Big Green Egg cooker temperature to 400 degrees F with convEGGtor.
2. Blend coconut oil with salt, sugar, baking powder, and flour in a food processor.
3. Transfer this flour mixture to a mixing bowl.
4. Now add coconut milk and lemon zest to the flour mixture, then mix well.
5. Fold in blueberries and mix the dough well until smooth.
6. Spread this blueberry dough into a 7-inch round and place it in a pan.
7. Refrigerate the blueberry dough for 15 minutes, then slice it into 6 wedges.
8. Layer the cooking pan with a parchment sheet.
9. Place the blueberry wedges in the lined cooking pan.
10. Bake in the preheated Big Green Egg Cooker for 25 minutes.
11. Serve fresh.

Nutritional Information per Serving:

- Calories 412
- Total Fat 24.8 g
- Saturated Fat 12.4 g
- Cholesterol 3 mg
- Sodium 132 mg
- Total Carbs 43.8 g
- Dietary Fiber 3.9 g
- Sugar 2.5 g
- Protein 18.9 g

Cream Soufflé

Serving: 2
Prep Time: 5 minutes
Cooking Time: 6 minutes

Ingredients:

- 1 fresh red chili pepper, chopped
- Salt, to taste
- 2 tablespoons light cream
- 2 eggs
- Green onions, chopped, to garnish

Method:

1. Adjust the Big Green Egg cooker temperature to 390 degrees F with convEGGtor.
2. Grease 2 soufflé dishes with cooking spray.
3. Whisk all of its ingredients together in a bowl.
4. Pour the mixture into the soufflé dishes.
5. Bake them for 6 minutes in the preheated Big Green Egg Cooker.
6. Garnish with green onions.
7. Serve with crispy bacon.

Nutritional Information per Serving:

- Calories 108
- Total Fat 9 g
- Saturated Fat 4.3 g
- Cholesterol 180 mg
- Sodium 146 mg
- Total Carbs 1.1 g
- Fiber 0.1 g
- Sugar 0.5 g
- Protein 6 g

Chapter 4: Snacks Recipes

Roasted Salsa

Serving: 6
Prep Time: 10 minutes
Cooking Time: 20 minutes

Ingredients:

- 2 bell peppers, quartered
- 4 beefsteak tomatoes, quartered
- 2 jalapeños, quartered
- 3 cloves garlic, diced
- 3 green onions, sliced
- 2 limes, sliced
- 1 bunch cilantro, chopped

Method:

1. Preheat the Big green egg cooker to 375 degrees F without the convEGGtor.
2. Arrange the sliced tomatoes, bell peppers, garlic, green onion, and jalapenos on the Big green egg cooker grill.
3. Grill the vegetables for 5-10 minutes per side until slightly charred.
4. Transfer the vegetables to a blender and add cilantro and lime juice.
5. Puree the mixture.
6. Serve with your favorite chips.

Nutritional Information per Serving:

- Calories 149
- Total Fat 11.9 g
- Saturated Fat 1.7 g
- Cholesterol 78 mg
- Sodium 79 mg
- Total Carbs 12.8 g
- Fiber 1.1 g
- Sugar 20.3 g
- Protein 5 g

Buffalo Cauliflower

Serving: 4
Prep Time: 10 minutes
Cooking Time: 20 minutes

Ingredients

- 1 large head cauliflower, cut into pieces
- 1 cup all-purpose flour
- 1 teaspoon vegan bouillon granules
- 1/4 teaspoon cayenne pepper
- 1/4 teaspoon chili powder
- 1/4 teaspoon paprika
- 1/4 teaspoon dried chipotle chili flakes
- 1 cup of soy milk
- canola oil spray
- 2 tablespoons nondairy butter
- 1/2 cup Cayenne Pepper Sauce
- 2 garlic cloves, minced

Method:

1. Preheat the Big green egg cooker to 350 degrees F with convEGGtor.
2. Whisk flour with cayenne, chili powder, bouillon granules, chipotle flakes, and paprika in a large bowl.
3. Gradually pour all the milk in and mix well until it forms a smooth batter.
4. Add the cauliflower pieces to the flour batter and mix to coat well.
5. Place these cauliflower pieces in a greased baking pan.
1. Bake them for 20 minutes in in the preheated Big Green Cooker.
6. Meanwhile, melt butter in a small-sized saucepan and add garlic and hot sauce.
7. Stir cook this mixture until it thickens.
8. Pour this sauce over the air fried cauliflower and serve warm.

Nutritional Information per Serving:

- Calories 101
- Total Fat 2.2 g
- Saturated Fat 2.4 g
- Cholesterol 110 mg
- Sodium 276 mg
- Total Carbs 25 g
- Fiber 1.4 g
- Sugar 1.4 g
- Protein 8.8 g

Smoked Mashed Potatoes

Serving: 2
Prep Time: 10 minutes
Cooking Time: 20 minutes

Ingredients:

- olive oil
- Sea salt and black pepper, to taste
- 1-1/2 pounds small red new potatoes
- 2 tablespoons butter, softened

Method:

1. Clean and pat dry the potatoes and place them in a sheet pan.
2. Rub the red potatoes with olive oil, salt, and pepper.
3. Preheat the Big green egg cooker to 350 degrees F with convEGGtor.
4. Place the potatoes on the Big green egg and cook for 20 minutes.
5. Once cooked, allow the potatoes and remove the skin.
6. Mash the potatoes in a bowl and fold in salt, pepper, and butter.
7. Serve and enjoy.

Nutritional Information per Serving:

- Calories 113
- Total Fat 4 g
- Saturated Fat 8 g
- Cholesterol 81 mg
- Sodium 162 mg
- Total Carbs 23 g
- Fiber 2.7 g
- Sugar 1 g
- Protein 2 g

Maple Glazed Smoked Pineapple

Serving: 2
Prep Time: 10 minutes
Cooking Time: 20 minutes

Ingredients:

- 1 whole pineapple, peeled and sliced into rings
- 2 to 3 tablespoons pure maple syrup
- 1 teaspoon kosher salt

Method:

1. Preheat the Big green egg cooker to 350 degrees F with convEGGtor.
2. Spread the pineapple rings on a sheet pan and pour the maple syrup on top.
3. Place the rings on the Big green egg cooker and sprinkle salt on top.
4. Return the rack to the Big green egg cooker.
5. Bake the rings for 20 minutes.
6. Serve.

Nutritional Information per Serving:

- Calories 179
- Total Fat 29.7 g
- Saturated Fat 8.6 g
- Cholesterol 141 mg
- Sodium 193 mg
- Total Carbs 23.7g
- Fiber 0.4 g
- Sugar 1.3 g
- Protein 0.2 g

Ranch Kale Chips

Serving: 6
Prep Time: 10 minutes
Cooking Time: 5 minutes

Ingredients

- 2 tablespoons olive oil
- 4 cups kale leaves
- 2 teaspoons Vegan Ranch Seasoning
- 1 tablespoon nutritional yeast flakes
- 1/4 teaspoon salt

Method:

2. Preheat the Big green egg cooker to 350 degrees F with convEGGtor.
3. Toss the kale leaves with oil, yeast, and Ranch seasoning in a large bowl.
4. Spread the seasoned kale leaves in the baking sheet.
5. Bake the kale leaves in the preheated Big Green Cooker for 5 minutes.
6. Serve warm.

Nutritional Information per Serving:

- Calories 113
- Total Fat 4 g
- Saturated Fat 8 g
- Cholesterol 81 mg
- Sodium 162 mg
- Total Carbs 13 g
- Fiber 2.7 g
- Sugar 1 g
- Protein 2 g

Cheese Sticks

Serving: 6
Prep Time: 10 minutes
Cooking Time: 10 minutes

Ingredients

- 6 cheese sticks
- 2 large eggs
- 1/4 cup whole wheat flour
- 1/4 cup parmesan cheese, grated
- 1 tsp Italian Seasoning
- 1 tsp garlic powder
- 1/4 tsp ground rosemary

Method:

1. Preheat the Big green egg cooker to 350 degrees F without convEGGtor.
2. Whisk eggs in a shallow bowl and keep it aside.
3. Mix flour with cheese and seasonings in another shallow bowl.
4. Dip the cheese sticks in the eggs and coat them with flour mixture.
5. Transfer these cheese sticks to the Air Fryer.
6. Grill the cheese sticks in the preheated Big Green Cooker for 5 minutes per side.
7. Serve warm.

Nutritional Information per Serving:

- Calories 179
- Total Fat 29.7 g
- Saturated Fat 8.6 g
- Cholesterol 141 mg
- Sodium 193 mg
- Total Carbs 13.7g
- Fiber 0.4 g
- Sugar 1.3 g
- Protein 10.2 g

Pork Stuffed Potatoes

Serving: 4
Prep Time: 10 minutes
Cooking Time: 30 minutes

Ingredients:

- 1/2 - 3/4 lb. pulled pork
- 2 russet potatoes
- 1/3 cup sour cream
- 4 oz. cream cheese
- 1/3 cup cheddar cheese
- ½ cup Chives, chopped
- BBQ sauce to taste

Method:

1. Preheat the Big green egg cooker to 325 degrees F without convEGGtor.
2. Place the potatoes in the Big green egg cooker for 30 minutes while rotating after every 5 minutes.
3. Slice each potato in half and scoop out its flesh from the center, leaving the skin intact.
4. Mix the potato flesh with cheddar cheese, cream cheese, sour cream, BBQ sauce and pulled pork in a bowl.
5. Spoon the potato mash into the potato skin.
6. Place the stuffed potatoes in the Big green egg cooker with convEGGtor and cook for 10 minutes.
7. Top them with cheddar cheese, chives and BBQ sauce.
8. Serve warm.

Nutritional Information per Serving:

- Calories 148
- Total Fat 22.4 g
- Saturated Fat 10.1 g
- Cholesterol 320 mg
- Sodium 350 mg
- Total Carbs 32.2 g
- Fiber 0.7 g
- Sugar 0.7 g
- Protein 4.3 g

Plantains Chips

Serving: 4
Prep Time: 10 minutes
Cooking Time: 10 minutes

Ingredients

- 2 ripe plantains, sliced
- 2 teaspoons avocado oil
- 1/8 teaspoon salt

Method:

1. Preheat the Big green egg cooker to 350 degrees F with convEGGtor.
2. Gently toss the plantains with oil and salt in a bowl.
3. Spread the chips in a baking sheet.
4. Bake the chips in the preheated Big Green Cooker for 5 minutes per side.
5. Serve fresh.

Nutritional Information per Serving:

- Calories 168
- Total Fat 6 g
- Saturated Fat 1.2 g
- Cholesterol 351 mg
- Sodium 103 mg
- Total Carbs 72.8 g
- Fiber 9.2 g
- Sugar 32.9 g
- Protein 7.2 g

Chapter 5: Poultry Recipes

Chicken Bake

Serving: 4
Prep Time: 10 minutes
Cooking Time: 40 minutes

Ingredients

- 1 can (14.5 oz.) canned tomatoes, diced
- 1 tablespoon olive oil
- 1 yellow onion, chopped
- 3 garlic cloves, minced
- 1 teaspoon dried oregano
- 1 teaspoon Italian seasoning
- 2 tablespoons chopped fresh parsley
- 4 boneless, skinless chicken breasts
- salt and fresh ground pepper, to taste
- 3/4 cup grated gruyere cheese
- 1 tbsp chopped fresh parsley, for garnish

Method:

1. Preheat the Big green egg cooker to 300 degrees F with convEGGtor.
2. Grease the baking dish with cooking spray.
3. Toss the tomatoes with olive oil, garlic, onions, Italian seasoning, oregano, and parsley in a bowl.
4. Spread this tomato mixture in the prepared baking dish.
5. Rub the chicken with salt, and black pepper then place over the tomatoes.
6. Bake the chicken in the preheated Green Egg Cooker for 35 minutes.
7. Drizzle the cheese over the chicken and bake for 5 minutes.
8. Serve warm.

Nutritional Information per Serving:

- Calories 297
- Total Fat 14 g
- Saturated Fat 5 g
- Cholesterol 99 mg
- Sodium 364 mg
- Total Carbs 8 g
- Fiber 1 g
- Sugar 3 g
- Protein 32 g

BBQ Chicken Wings

Serving: 8
Prep Time: 10 minutes
Cooking Time: 2 hrs. 10 minutes

Ingredients:

For the wings:

- 4 lbs. chicken wings without tips, drumettes, and flats separated
- 3 tablespoons paprika
- 1 tablespoon chilli powder
- 4 teaspoons kosher salt
- 1 tablespoon onion powder
- 1 tablespoon garlic powder
- 1 teaspoon mustard powder
- 1 teaspoon chipotle Chile powder

For the barbecue sauce

- 1 tablespoon barbecue sauce
- 2 tablespoons butter (unsalted)
- 1 tablespoon. mild-flavoured molasses
- 1 tablespoon Texas Pete hot sauce
- kosher salt, to taste

Method:

1. Preheat the Big green egg cooker to 225 degrees F with convEGGtor.
2. Meanwhile, mix and whisk all the spices in a small bowl.
3. Place the wings in a sheet pan and rub of the spice mixture on both sides of the wings.
4. Let them marinate for 15 to 20 minutes.
5. Place the wings in the Big green egg cooker and smoke until their internal temperature reaches to 160F.
6. Mix all the BBQ sauce ingredients in a saucepan and cook until it thickens.
7. Brush the wings with the BBQ sauce on both sides and smoke for another 5 to 10 minutes.
8. Serve warm.

Nutritional Information per Serving:

- Calories 380
- Total Fat 20 g
- Saturated Fat 5 g
- Cholesterol 151 mg
- Sodium 686 mg
- Total Carbs 33 g
- Fiber 1 g
- Sugar 1.2 g
- Protein 21 g

Orange Stuffed Turkey

Serving: 8
Prep Time: 10 minutes
Cooking Time: 6 ½ hours

Ingredients:

- 1 (12 to 14 pounds) whole turkey, cleaned
- 2 tablespoons dried thyme
- 1 tablespoon powdered sage
- 2 teaspoons dried oregano
- 2 teaspoons paprika
- 2 teaspoons sea salt
- 1-1/2 teaspoons cracked black pepper
- 1 teaspoon dried rosemary
- 1 teaspoon onion or garlic powder
- zest of 1/2 an orange
- 1/4 cup extra-virgin olive oil

Method:

1. Preheat the Big green egg cooker to 225 degrees F with convEGGtor.
2. Mix spices and dry herbs in a small bowl.
3. Rub the turkey from inside with 1/3 of the seasoning liberally.
4. Whisk the remaining seasoning with the olive oil and orange zest.
5. Rub this mixture over the turkey. Tuck the turkey wings beneath it.
6. Place the turkey in the Big green egg cooker.
7. Cover the lid and cook for 6 and a 1/2 hours.
8. Let it smoke until the internal temperature reaches 165 degrees F.
9. Once cooked, remove the turkey and let it rest for 20 minutes.
10. Carve and serve.

Nutritional Information per Serving:

- Calories 352
- Total Fat 14 g
- Saturated Fat 2 g
- Cholesterol 65 mg
- Sodium 220 mg
- Total Carbs 15.8 g
- Fiber 0.2 g
- Sugar 1 g
- Protein 26 g

Thanksgiving Turkey

Serving: 8
Prep Time: 10 minutes
Cooking Time: 6 and 1/2 hours

Ingredients:

- 1 (12 to 14 pound) whole turkey
- 3 tablespoons olive oil
- 3 tablespoons unsalted butter
- 2 cloves fresh garlic minced
- 2 tablespoons dried thyme
- 1 tablespoon powdered sage
- 2 teaspoons dried oregano
- 2 teaspoons paprika
- 2 teaspoons sea salt
- 1-1/2 teaspoons cracked black pepper
- 1 teaspoon dried rosemary
- 1 apple cut in quarters
- 1 lemon or orange cut in quarters
- 1 medium onion cut in half

Method:

1. Preheat the Big green egg cooker to 300 degrees F with convEGGtor.
2. Mix all the spices, herbs, garlic, softened butter and olive oil.
3. Rub the turkey inside with 1/3 of this mixture.
4. Add onion and fruits to the cavity of turkey.
5. Coat the outside with the remaining mixture and fat.
6. Tuck the wings of the turkey and place it on with its fat side up.
7. Insert the digital thermometer into the meat and place in the cooker
8. Cover the lid and let it smoke for 6 and 1/2 hours.
9. Cook until the thermometer reaches to 165 degrees F.
10. Allow the cooked meat to rest for 20 minutes.
11. Slice and serve.

Nutritional Information per Serving:

- Calories 231
- Total Fat 20.1 g
- Saturated Fat 2.4 g
- Cholesterol 110 mg
- Sodium 941 mg
- Total Carbs 30.1 g
- Fiber 0.9 g
- Sugar 1.4 g
- Protein 14.6 g

Sesame Chicken Tenders

Serving: 6
Prep Time: 10 minutes
Cooking Time: 1hour

Ingredients:

- 4 lbs. chicken tenders rinsed and patted dry
- ½ cup soy sauce
- ½ cup vegetable oil
- ¼ cup water
- 1 ½ tablespoon sesame seeds
- 2 teaspoons minced garlic
- ¾ teaspoon freshly grated peeled ginger root
- ¼ teaspoon Cajun seasoning
- jane's Krazy mixed-up salt, to taste

Method:

1. Preheat the Big green egg cooker to 225 degrees F with convEGGtor.
2. Mix sesame seeds, vegetable oil, soy sauce, Cajun seasoning, Krazy salt and water in a bowl.
3. Place the tenders in the Ziplock bag and pour the spice mixture into it. Shake well.
4. Seal the bags and refrigerate for 8 hours.
5. Remove the tenders from the marinade and place them in the Big green egg cooker.
6. Cook for 1 hour until al dente.
7. Serve warm.

Nutritional Information per Serving:

- Calories 301
- Total Fat 15.8 g
- Saturated Fat 2.7 g
- Cholesterol 75 mg
- Sodium 189 mg
- Total Carbs 31.7 g
- Fiber 0.3 g
- Sugar 0.1 g
- Protein 28.2 g

Stuffed Smoked Hens

Serving: 10
Prep Time: 10 minutes
Cooking Time: 2 ½ hours

Ingredients:

- 4 whole Cornish game hens
- 1/4 cup extra-virgin olive oil
- 3 oranges cut into quarters
- 4 teaspoon sea salt
- 2 teaspoon cracked black pepper
- 2 teaspoon dried thyme

Method:

1. Preheat the Big green egg cooker to 250 degrees F with convEGGtor.
2. Rinse and pat dry the hens.
3. Let the hens rest at room temperature for about 30 minutes.
4. Mix olive oil with seasonings in a bowl.
5. Coat the hens with seasoning mixture from inside and out.
6. Stuff the hens with 3 orange quarters. Tie the legs using a butcher's wine.
7. Place the hens in the Big green egg cooker.
8. Cook for 2 hours 30 minutes until internal temperature reaches to 165 degrees F.
9. Cover the hens with foil and let them rest for 15 to 20 minutes.
10. Slice in half and remove the oranges.
11. Serve warm.

Nutritional Information per Serving:

- Calories 440
- Total Fat 7.9 g
- Saturated Fat 1.8 g
- Cholesterol 5 mg
- Sodium 581 mg
- Total Carbs 21.8 g
- Sugar 7.1 g
- Fiber 2.6 g
- Protein 37.2 g

Rosemary Turkey Breast

Serving: 10
Prep Time: 10 minutes
Cooking Time: 4hours 5 minutes

Ingredients:

- 1 (64-oz.) bottle apple cider
- 3/4 cup kosher salt
- 1/2 cup sugar
- 1/4 cup apple cider vinegar
- 3 (4-inch) fresh thyme sprigs
- 2 (4-inch) fresh rosemary sprigs
- 10 fresh sage leaves
- 1 garlic bulb, cut in half crosswise
- 4 cups ice cubes
- 1 (5 3/4- to 6-lb.) bone-in turkey breast
- 4 hickory wood chunks

Method:

1. Preheat the Big green egg cooker to 225 degrees F with convEGGtor
2. Add cider, vinegar, salt, and sugar, sprigs, sage and garlic bulb to a stockpot.
3. Bring this vinegar mixture to a boil over medium-high heat.
4. Reduce the heat to medium and let it simmer for 5 minutes.
5. Remove the mixture from the heat and add ice cubes.
6. Place the turkey in the brine and cover it. Refrigerate for 12 hours.
7. Remove the turkey from the brine and pat it dry with the paper towel.
8. Place the turkey in the Big green egg cooker and cook for 4 hours.
9. Slice and serve.

Nutritional Information per Serving:

- Calories 297
- Total Fat 14 g
- Saturated Fat 5 g
- Cholesterol 99 mg
- Sodium 364 mg
- Total Carbs 8 g
- Fiber 1 g
- Sugar 3 g
- Protein 32 g

Chicken Tenderloins

Serving: 4
Prep Time: 10 minutes
Cooking Time: 12 minutes

Ingredients

- 1 egg
- ½ cup dry bread crumbs
- 2 tablespoons vegetable oil
- 8 chicken tenderloins

Method:

1. Preheat the Big green egg cooker to 350 degrees F with convEGGtor.
2. Whisk egg in a bowl and mix crumbs with oil in another bowl.
3. First, dip the chicken in the egg then coat well with crumbs mixture.
4. Bake the chicken in the preheated Green Egg Cooker for 6 minutes per side.
5. Serve warm.

Nutritional Information per Serving:

- Calories 352
- Total Fat 14 g
- Saturated Fat 2 g
- Cholesterol 65 mg
- Sodium 220 mg
- Total Carbs 15.8 g
- Fiber 0.2 g
- Sugar 1 g
- Protein 26 g

Mandarin Stuffed Duck

Serving: 6
Prep Time: 10 minutes
Cooking Time: 4 hours

Ingredients:

- 6 lb. whole duck, cleaned
- 2 tablespoons honey
- 1 small onion, quartered

- 1 tablespoon soy sauce
- 2 small mandarin oranges, quartered
- Pepper and salt to taste

For Glaze

- 1 tablespoon molasses
- 1 tablespoon honey
- 1 tablespoon balsamic vinegar

- 2 tablespoons orange juice
- Zest of 1 orange
- Pinch of pepper and salt

Method:

1. Preheat the Big green egg cooker to 325 degrees F with convEGGtor.
2. Wash and pat dry the duck from the inside and out.
3. Score the duck's skin using a fork or a sharp knife.
4. Brush the duck with soy sauce, honey, pepper and salt.
5. Stuff the duck with onion and mandarin.
6. Refrigerate the duck overnight for marination.
7. Mix all the ingredients for glaze in a bowl.
8. Brush the marinated duck with the prepared glaze.
9. Place the prepared duck on the Big green egg cooker rack and smoke until the meat is al dente.
10. Serve warm.

Nutritional Information per Serving:

- Calories 361
- Total Fat 16.3 g
- Saturated Fat 4.9 g
- Cholesterol 114 mg
- Sodium 515 mg

- Total Carbs 19.3 g
- Fiber 0.1 g
- Sugar 18.2 g
- Protein 33.3 g

Chapter 6: Beef, Lamb and Pork Recipes

Smoked Tri-Tip Roast

Serving: 4
Prep Time: 10 minutes
Cooking Time: 2 hours

Ingredients:

- 1 (2 to 3) pound tri-tip roast
- 2 teaspoons sea salt
- 1-1/2 teaspoons mild chilli powder
- 1 teaspoon black pepper
- 1 teaspoon brown sugar
- 1 teaspoon espresso powder
- 1 teaspoon onion powder
- 1/2 teaspoon garlic powder

Method:

1. Preheat the Big green egg cooker to 225 degrees F with convEGGtor.
2. Mix and whisk all the spices together in a small bowl.
3. Score the roast using a sharp knife in diagonal patterns.
4. Rub the spice mixture over the roast generously. Let it marinate for 90 minutes at room temperature.
5. Arrange the roast in the Big green egg cooker.
6. Smoke the roast for 2 hours until its internal temperature reaches to 135 degrees.
7. Carve and serve.

Nutritional Information per Serving:

- Calories 301
- Total Fat 15.8 g
- Saturated Fat 2.7 g
- Cholesterol 75 mg
- Sodium 389 mg
- Total Carbs 11.7 g
- Fiber 0.3g
- Sugar 0.1 g
- Protein 28.2 g

Tangy Smoked Ham

Serving: 8
Prep Time: 10 minutes
Cooking Time: 45 minutes

Ingredients:

- 1/4 cup honey
- ¼ cup dark brown sugar
- 1 tablespoon Dijon mustard
- 10 lbs. precooked ham, butt portion
- 2 tablespoons whole cloves
- 8 oz. Cajun butter
- hickory (chips)

Method:

1. Preheat the Big green egg cooker to 225 degrees F with convEGGtor.
2. Mix mustard with honey and brown sugar in a bowl.
3. Add ham to the bowl and mix well to coat.
4. Carve a 5 to the 3-inch deep slit in the ham and stuff it with cloves.
5. Add Cajun butter to the ham and let it marinate for 1 hour.
6. Smoke the marinated ham in the Big green egg cooker and cook for 45 minutes.
7. Pour the remaining marinade on top and serve.

Nutritional Information per Serving:

- Calories 548
- Total Fat 22.9 g
- Saturated Fat 9 g
- Cholesterol 105 mg
- Sodium 350 mg
- Total Carbs 17.5 g
- Sugar 10.9 g
- Fiber 6.3 g
- Protein 40.1 g

Pepper Pork Shoulder

Serving: 6
Prep Time: 10 minutes
Cooking Time: 4 hours

Ingredients:

- 4 lbs. pork shoulder
- 2 tablespoons kosher salt
- 2½ tablespoons smoked paprika
- 2½ tablespoons lemon pepper
- 1 tablespoon cayenne pepper
- 1 tablespoon smoked garlic powder
- ½ tablespoon ground black pepper
- ½ cup yellow mustard
- 2-3 tablespoons Worcestershire sauce
- plastic wrap
- ½ cup apple cider vinegar
- ½ cup apple juice
- ½ cup water
- 2 cups hickory smoking chips
- 2 cups mesquite smoking chips

Method:

1. Rinse and pat dry the cleaned pork shoulder with a paper towel.
2. Mix all the dry spices in a small bowl.
3. Place the pork should in a sheet pan.
4. Pour the Worcestershire sauce over the pork shoulder and rub well.
5. Add mustard on top and spread it thoroughly.
6. Sprinkle the spice mixture over the pork shoulder.
7. Wrap the pork shoulder with plastic wrap and refrigerate for 12 hours.
8. Preheat the Big green egg cooker to 250 degrees F with convEGGtor.
9. Smoke the pork for about 4 hours until the internal temperature reaches to 165 degrees.
10. Let it rest at room temperature for 5 to 10 minutes.
11. Serve.

Nutritional Information per Serving:

- Calories 301
- Total Fat 8.9 g
- Saturated Fat 4.5 g
- Cholesterol 57 mg
- Sodium 340 mg
- Total Carbs 24.7 g
- Fiber 1.2 g
- Sugar 1.3 g
- Protein 15.3 g

Indian Spiced Pork Roast

Serving: 6
Prep Time: 10 minutes
Cooking Time: 2 hours

Ingredients:

- 4-star anise
- 1 teaspoon cumin
- 1 teaspoon coriander
- 1/2 teaspoon cardamom seeds
- 1/2 teaspoon black peppercorns
- 1 teaspoon turmeric, powdered
- ½ teaspoon red Chile, ground
- salt, to taste
- 4 tablespoons canola oil
- 6 lbs. roast pork

Method:

1. Preheat the Big green egg cooker to 250 degrees F with convEGGtor.
2. Ground and blend all the spices in a food processor,
3. Rub the pork roast with oil and all the spices, cover and marinate for 20 minutes.
4. Cook for 2 hours in the preheated Green Egg cooker.
5. Serve.

Nutritional Information per Serving:

- Calories 609
- Total Fat 50.5 g
- Saturated Fat 11.7 g
- Cholesterol 58 mg
- Sodium 463 mg
- Total Carbs 9.9 g
- Fiber 1.5 g
- Sugar 0.3 g
- Protein 29.3 g

Spicy Pork with Pintos

Serving: 4
Prep Time: 10 minutes
Cooking Time: 4 hours

Ingredients:

- 4lbs. Boneless pork country style ribs
- 3 cans Pinto beans
- 10 oz. jar Hot pepper jelly
- 1 cup BBQ sauce
- 2 cups onions, chopped
- 3 cloves garlic, chopped
- Salt, to taste
- Black Pepper, to taste
- Cayenne, to taste

Method:

1. Preheat the Big green egg cooker to 200 degrees F with convEGGtor.
2. Mix salt, black pepper and cayenne in a bowl.
3. Season the ribs with spice mixture.
4. Place the ribs in a sheet pan and place it in the middle rack of the Big green egg cooker.
5. Cook for 1 1/2 hours in the preheated Green Egg cooker.
6. Meanwhile, mix beans with BBQ sauce, garlic, onion and pepper jelly in a bowl.
7. Pour the beans mixture over the ribs and cover them with a foil.
8. Cook the ribs for another 3 to 4 hours at 250 degrees F.
9. Remove the foil and smoke for another 30 minutes.
10. Serve.

Nutritional Information per Serving:

- Calories 537
- Total Fat 19.8 g
- Saturated Fat 1.4 g
- Cholesterol 10 mg
- Sodium 719 mg
- Total Carbs 25.1 g
- Fiber 0.9 g
- Sugar 1.4 g
- Protein 37.8 g

Spicy Barbeque Meatloaf

Serving: 6
Prep Time: 10 minutes
Cooking Time: 2 hrs. 15 minutes

Ingredients:

- 1 lb. ground beef
- ½ lb. ground veal
- ½ lb. ground pork
- 1 tablespoon olive oil
- 1 yellow onion, finely chopped
- 1 cup small pieces of white bread
- 2 teaspoons Barbecue sauce
- 4 oz. whole milk
- 1 tablespoon Worcestershire sauce
- ¼ cup Parmesan cheese, grated
- 1 tablespoon mustard
- 1 tablespoon salt
- hickory chips, soaked
- 2 tablespoon spice mixture

For spice mixture

- 1 tablespoon Cayenne pepper
- ½ white pepper
- ½ black pepper
- 1 teaspoon paprika
- ½ teaspoon salt
- ½ teaspoon onion powder
- ½ teaspoon garlic powder
- ¼ teaspoon dried oregano
- ¼ teaspoon dried thyme
- 1/8 teaspoon ground coriander
- ¼ ground cumin
- 1/8 teaspoon mustard, dry
- 1/12 teaspoon salt, celery

Method:

1. Preheat the Big green egg cooker to 225 degrees F with convEGGtor.
2. Preheat the Big green egg cooker to 225 degrees F.
3. Let the prepared meat rest at room temperature for 30 minutes.
4. Heat olive oil in a skillet over medium heat and add onion to sauté for 10 minutes.
5. Turn off the heat and set it aside.
6. Mix milk with bread in a bowl and let it rest for 3 minutes.
7. Whisk eggs with sautéed onion, milk-soaked the bread, mustard salt, BBQ sauce, parmesan, Worcestershire sauce and spice mixture in a bowl.
8. Add ground meat to the mixture and mix well.
9. Transfer the mixture to a loaf pan and press it firmly.
10. Place the loaf pan in the Big green egg cooker and cover the lid.
11. Let it smoke for 1 to 2 hours until meat is done.
12. Slice and serve warm.

Nutritional Information per Serving:

- Calories 472
- Total Fat 11.1 g
- Saturated Fat 5.8 g
- Cholesterol 610 mg
- Sodium 749 mg
- Total Carbs 19.9 g
- Fiber 0.2 g
- Sugar 0.2 g
- Protein 13.5 g

Glazed Ham

Serving: 8
Prep Time: 10 minutes
Cooking Time: 3 hours

Ingredients:

- 1 (10 to 16) pound bone-in baked ham shoulder
- 1/2 cup pure maple syrup
- 1/2 cup cane sugar
- 1/4 cup sweet apple cider or pineapple juice
- 2 tablespoons spicy brown mustard

Method:

1. Preheat the Big green egg cooker to 250 degrees F with convEGGtor.
2. Rinse and pat dry the ham.
3. Place the ham on a sheet pan with its flat side down. Let it rest for 30 to 45 minutes.
4. Transfer the ham to the lower section of the Big green egg cooker and cook for 60 to 90 minutes.
5. Meanwhile, add the remaining ingredients to a saucepan.
6. Mix well and cook this mixture until it thickens.
7. Once ham is cooked, generously coat it with prepared from both the sides.
8. Smoked again for 60 to 90 minutes.
9. Transfer the ham to the cutting board and let it rest for 15 minutes under the foil.
10. Serve warm.

Nutritional Information per Serving:

- Calories 392
- Total Fat 16.1 g
- Saturated Fat 2.3 g
- Cholesterol 231 mg
- Sodium 466 mg
- Total Carbs 3.9 g
- Sugar 0.6 g
- Fiber 0.9 g
- Protein 48 g

Dijon Smoked Brisket

Serving: 8
Prep Time: 10 minutes
Cooking Time: 12 hours

Ingredients:

- 8-10 lb. brisket
- 2 tablespoons paprika
- 2 tablespoons garlic powder
- 2 tablespoons onion powder
- 2 tablespoons brown sugar
- 2 tablespoons kosher salt
- 2 tablespoons black pepper
- 1 tablespoon cayenne pepper
- 1 tablespoon cumin
- 1 tablespoon red pepper flakes
- Dijon mustard
- Worcestershire sauce
- 5 oz. apple juice

Method:

1. Preheat the Big green egg cooker to 225 degrees F with convEGGtor.
2. Clean the briskets and remove the excess fats.
3. Blend all the dry spices together in a bowl.
4. Coat the briskets with Worcestershire sauce and Dijon mustard.
5. Rub the coated briskets with dry rub mixture.
6. Smoke the briskets in the Big green egg cooker for 8 hours.
7. Wrap the brisket with apple juice in an aluminium foil.
8. Return the brisket to the Big green egg cooker and smoke for another 4 hours.
9. Once cooked, allow it to cool then slice.
10. Serve.

Nutritional Information per Serving:

- Calories 452
- Total Fat 4 g
- Saturated Fat 2 g
- Cholesterol 65 mg
- Sodium 220 mg
- Total Carbs 23.1 g
- Fiber 0.3 g
- Sugar 1 g
- Protein 26g

Spicy Baby Ribs

Serving: 4
Prep Time: 10 minutes
Cooking Time: 4.5 hours

Ingredients:

- 2 slabs of baby back ribs
- 1/2 cup brown sugar
- 1/4 cup smoked paprika
- 1/2 teaspoon chilli powder
- 1-1/2 tablespoon kosher salt
- 1 tablespoon ground black pepper
- 2 teaspoons garlic powder
- 2 teaspoons onion powder

Method:

1. Preheat the Big green egg cooker to 225 degrees F with convEGGtor.
2. Remove the membrane and pat the dry the ribs
3. Mix all the dry seasoning and rub it over the ribs. Let it rest for 30 minutes.
4. Place the seasoned ribs in the Big green egg cooker with their meat side up
5. Let it smoke for 3 hours.
6. Transfer the rack of ribs over 2 sheets of foil and pour a basting liquid of your choice.
7. Wrap the foil completely around the rack.
8. Return the ribs to the Big green egg cooker and cook for another 1 to 1 1/2 hours until its internal temperature reaches to 160 degrees.
9. Serve warm.

Nutritional Information per Serving:

- Calories 457
- Total Fat 19.1 g
- Saturated Fat 11 g
- Cholesterol 262 mg
- Sodium 557 mg
- Total Carbs 18.9 g
- Sugar 1.2 g
- Fiber 1.7 g
- Protein 32.5 g

Five Spice Pork Lion

Serving: 6
Prep Time: 10 minutes
Cooking Time: 3 hours

Ingredients:

- 4 pounds boneless pork loin, whole
- 2 teaspoons sea salt
- 1 tablespoon Chinese five-spice powder
- 1 teaspoon black pepper, cracked
- ¼ teaspoon nutmeg
- ½ teaspoon garlic powder
- 2 tablespoons Safflower or grapeseed oil
- Apple juice, unsweetened

Method:

1. Preheat the Big green egg cooker to 255 degrees F with convEGGtor.
2. Rinse and pat dry the cleaned pork loin with a paper towel. Trim off excess fats.
3. Mix all the herbs, oil and spices in a bowl.
4. Rub the pork loin with the spice mixture thoroughly.
5. Let it marinate for 60 minutes at room temperature.
6. Arrange the pork loin on the Big green egg cooker.
7. Cook for approximately 3 hours until meat's internal temperature reaches 155 degrees F.
8. Serve warm.

Nutritional Information per Serving:

- Calories 353
- Total Fat 7.5 g
- Saturated Fat 1.1 g
- Cholesterol 20 mg
- Sodium 297 mg
- Total Carbs 10.4 g
- Fiber 0.2 g
- Sugar 0.1 g
- Protein 13.1 g

Mustard Dipped Boston Roast

Serving: 8
Prep Time: 10 minutes
Cooking Time: 8 hours

Ingredients:

- 8 pounds bone-in Boston butt roast
- 5 tablespoons jarred yellow mustard
- 1/3 cup packed brown sugar
- 3 tablespoons sea salt
- 2 tablespoons paprika
- 1 tablespoon garlic powder
- 1 tablespoon onion powder
- 2 teaspoons cracked black pepper
- 1/2 teaspoon cayenne pepper

Method:

1. Preheat the Big green egg cooker to 225 degrees F with convEGGtor.
2. Wash the roast and trim off its excess fat. Rinse and pat it dry.
3. Mix and whisk the ingredients for the dry rub in a bowl.
4. Brush the mustard liberally over the roast.
5. Rub the prepared roast with the spice mixture generously and liberally.
6. Place the prepared roast in a sheet pan and cover it with a plastic sheet.
7. Put in the refrigerator for 8 to 12 hours or overnight.
8. Set the roast in the Big green egg cooker.
9. Let it smoke for 8 hours and baste it with olive oil and remaining marinade.
10. Allow the roast to sit at room temperature for 30 minutes.
11. When cooled, pull the pork using 2 forks.
12. Serve warm and enjoy.

Nutritional Information per Serving:

- Calories 308
- Total Fat 20.5 g
- Saturated Fat 3 g
- Cholesterol 42 mg
- Sodium 688 mg
- Total Carbs 40.3 g
- Sugar 1.4 g
- Fiber 4.3 g
- Protein 49 g

Sweet Meat Jerky

Serving: 4
Prep Time: 10 minutes
Cooking Time: 3 hours

Ingredients:

- 1 lb. London broil, trimmed of fat, cut into 1/4-inch strips
- 3/4 cup unfiltered apple cider vinegar
- 2 tablespoons sea salt
- 2 tablespoons brown sugar
- 2 tablespoons blackstrap molasses
- 1 tablespoon cracked black pepper
- 1 teaspoon garlic powder
- 1 teaspoon onion powder
- 1 bottle stout or dark beer

Method:

1. Preheat the Big green egg cooker to 2250 degrees F without convEGGtor.
2. Keep the London broil in the freezer for 30 minutes.
3. Mix and whisk all the remaining ingredients in a bowl. Add only half of the beer while mixing.
4. Slice the frozen London broil into quarter inch strips.
5. Arrange these slices in a baking dish and pour the prepared marinade over the slices.
6. Cover the dish and let them marinate for 4 to 8 hours.
7. Remove the marinated meat slices from the marinade and pat them dry with paper towel.
8. Arrange the beef slices on the Big green egg cooker and cook for 3 hours.
9. Allow the beef jerky to cool then enjoy.

Nutritional Information per Serving:

- Calories 231
- Total Fat 20.1 g
- Saturated Fat 2.4 g
- Cholesterol 110 mg
- Sodium 941 mg
- Total Carbs 20.1 g
- Fiber 0.9 g
- Sugar 1.4 g
- Protein 14.6 g

Brine Pork Chops

Serving: 4
Prep Time: 10 minutes
Cooking Time: 30 minutes

Ingredients:

- 4 bone-in pork loin chops

For the brine:

- 1-gallon water
- Kosher salt, to taste
- ½ cup Granulated sugar
- 1 tablespoon peppercorn

For the rub:

- ¼ cup brown sugar
- 1 teaspoon onion powder
- 1 tablespoon chilli powder
- 1 teaspoon garlic powder
- 1 teaspoon cumin
- 2 teaspoon kosher salt
- 1 teaspoon paprika
- ½ teaspoon ground black pepper

Method:

1. Mix and whisk the ingredients for the brine in a saucepan and add water.
2. Bring the mixture to a boil and mix well until sugar is completely dissolved.
3. Allow the brine to cool then submerge the chops for 6 to 8 hours.
4. Mix all the ingredients for the rub in a bowl.
5. Remove the prepared chops from the brine and pat them dry.
6. Rub each chop with spice rub generously.
7. Preheat the Big green egg cooker to 200 degrees F with convEGGtor.
8. Place the chops in the Big green egg cooker and smoke for 30 minutes.
9. Reduce the heat and smoke until well cooked.
10. Serve warm.

Nutritional Information per Serving:

- Calories 327
- Total Fat 3.5 g
- Saturated Fat 0.5 g
- Cholesterol 162 mg
- Sodium 142 mg
- Total Carbs 33.6 g
- Fiber 0.4 g
- Sugar 0.5 g
- Protein 24.5 g

Pork Redneck Ribs

Serving: 4
Prep Time: 10 minutes
Cooking Time: 2 hours

Ingredients:

Ribs:

- 4 pounds country-style pork ribs
- 1 teaspoon of salt
- 1 teaspoon freshly ground black pepper
- 1/2 teaspoon onion powder
- 1/2 teaspoon garlic powder

BBQ Sauce:

- 1 cup ketchup
- 3/4 cup apple jelly
- 1/2 cup steak sauce
- 1/4 cup packed brown sugar

Method:

1. Preheat the Big green egg cooker to 250 degrees F with convEGGtor.
2. Mix garlic powder, salt, pepper and onion powder in a bowl.
3. Rub the ribs with the spice mixture.
4. Place the prepared ribs in the Big green egg cooker and cook for 1 hour.
5. Mix apple jelly with steak sauce, brown sugar, and ketchup in a saucepan.
6. Cook until the mixture is well combined.
7. Baste the smoked ribs with the prepared sauce.
8. Wrap the ribs with aluminium foil and return them to a Big green egg cooker.
9. Smoke the ribs for another 2 hours.
10. Serve warm with the remaining sauce.

Nutritional Information per Serving:

- Calories 545
- Total Fat 36.4 g
- Saturated Fat 10.1 g
- Cholesterol 200 mg
- Sodium 272 mg
- Total Carbs 40.7 g
- Fiber 0.2 g
- Sugar 0.1 g
- Protein 42.5 g

Earthy Pulled Pork

Serving: 10
Prep Time: 10 minutes
Cooking Time: 8 hrs

Ingredients:

- 1 (8 lb.) bone-in pork butt
- 9 x 13-inch aluminium tray
- 2 tablespoons coarse salt
- 2 tablespoons black pepper
- 1 tablespoon garlic powder
- 1 tablespoon onion powder
- 1 tablespoon chilli powder
- 1 tablespoon paprika
- ½ tablespoon cayenne pepper
- 4 tablespoons brown sugar

Method:

1. Preheat the Big green egg cooker to 250 degrees F with convEGGtor.
2. Place the pork butt in the aluminium tray.
3. Blend all the remaining ingredients together in a bowl.
4. Pour this mixture over the pork and mix well to coat.
5. Place the aluminium tray in the Big green egg cooker and cook for 1 hour per pound.
6. Once cooked, wrap the pork in aluminium foil. Let it rest for 15 minutes.
7. Pull the pork using two forks.
8. Serve warm.

Nutritional Information per Serving:

- Calories 248
- Total Fat 13 g
- Saturated Fat 7 g
- Cholesterol 387 mg
- Sodium 353 mg
- Total Carbs 21 g
- Fiber 0.4 g
- Sugar 1 g
- Protein 29 g

Chapter 7: Seafood Recipes

Soy Garlic Oysters

Serving: 6
Prep Time: 10 minutes
Cooking Time: 10 minutes

Ingredients:

- 1 lb. medium-sized oysters
- Salt, to taste
- ½ cup brown sugar
- ½ cup soy sauce
- 1 tablespoon of garlic powder
- 1 cup brandy
- Paper grinder
- Add hot sauce as desired
- 1 tablespoon dried chopped white onion

Method:

1. Preheat the Big green egg cooker to 350 degrees F with convEGGtor.
2. Mix and whisk the ingredients other than oysters in a saucepan.
3. Soak the oysters in the prepared mixture and refrigerate overnight.
4. Remove the oysters from the brine and rinse under clean water.
5. Place the oysters on the greased Big green egg cooker's rack.
6. Cook the oysters in the preheated Green Egg cooker for 10 minutes.
7. Mix garlic, red chilli and lemon zest in a bowl.
8. Pour this mixture over the smoked oysters.
9. Serve and enjoy.

Nutritional Information per Serving:

- Calories 378
- Total Fat 7 g
- Saturated Fat 8.1 g
- Cholesterol 230 mg
- Sodium 316 mg
- Total Carbs 16.2 g
- Sugar 0.2 g
- Fiber 0.3 g
- Protein 26 g

Halibut with Tartar Sauce

Serving: 4
Prep Time: 10 minutes
Cooking Time: 20 minutes

Ingredients:

- ¼ cup granulated sugar
- ¼ cup brown sugar
- ½ cup kosher salt

Homemade Tartar Sauce:

- 2 tablespoons minced white onion
- ¼ cup diced tomatoes
- 2 tablespoons diced dill pickle

- 1 teaspoon ground coriander
- 2 lbs. fresh halibut

- ½ cup mayonnaise
- 2 teaspoons vinegar
- salt to taste

Method:

1. Preheat the Big green egg cooker to 350 degrees F with convEGGtor.
2. Wash and rinse the fish thoroughly with water then pat it dry with paper towel.
3. Place this fish in a Ziplock bag and add all the ingredients for the marinade.
4. Shake and place the sealed fish bag in the refrigerator for 4 hours.
5. Remove the fish from the bag and pat it dry.
6. Place the fish in a sheet pan and refrigerate for another 2 hours.
7. Set the fish sheet pan in the Big green egg cooker and cook until it's until temperature reaches to 140 degrees F.
8. Serve warm

Nutritional Information per Serving:

- Calories 378
- Total Fat 21 g
- Saturated Fat 4.3 g
- Cholesterol 150 mg
- Sodium 146 mg

- Total Carbs 7.1 g
- Sugar 0.1 g
- Fiber 0.4 g
- Protein 23 g

Honey Glazed Sardines

Serving: 4
Prep Time: 10 minutes
Cooking Time: 20 minutes

Ingredients:

- 4 fresh sardines, gutted
- 4 cups water
- ¼ cup salt kosher
- ¼ cup honey
- 4 to 5 bay leaves
- 1 onion, chopped finely
- 2 garlic cloves, smashed
- ½ cup cilantro or parsley, chopped
- 3 to 4 hot chiles, dried and crushed
- 2 tablespoons peppercorns

Method:

1. Preheat the Big green egg cooker to 350 degrees F without convEGGtor.
2. Clean and wash the sardines and remove its backbone and ribs.
3. Add all the remaining ingredients to a saucepan and bring it to a boil.
4. Mix well and turn off the heat. Cover and allow it to cool.
5. Submerge the cleaned sardines in the prepared brine.
6. Refrigerate for about 12 hours.
7. Remove the fish from the brine and pat it dry using a paper towel.
8. Place the fish in the Big green egg cooker.
9. Cook the fish in the preheated Green Egg cooker for 10 minutes per side.
10. Serve warm.

Nutritional Information per Serving:

- Calories 248
- Total Fat 15.7 g
- Saturated Fat 2.7 g
- Cholesterol 75 mg
- Sodium 94 mg
- Total Carbs 31.4 g
- Fiber 0.4 g
- Sugar 3.1 g
- Protein 24.9 g

Smoked Oysters

Serving: 6
Prep Time: 10 minutes
Cooking Time: 20 minutes

Ingredients:

- 12 oysters
- 4 strips bacon
- 3 tablespoons fresh parsley, finely chopped
- 3 tablespoons butter, melted and cooled
- 3 tablespoons breadcrumbs
- 3 tablespoons Parmesan cheese, freshly grated

Method:

1. Preheat the Big green egg cooker to 350 degrees F with convEGGtor.
2. Cook the oysters in the preheated Green Egg cooker for 10 minutes.
3. Return the oysters to the pan and set them aside.
4. Grill bacon in the Big green egg cooker until brown and crispy from both the sides.
5. Mix the crispy bacon with parsley and top the oysters with this mixture.
6. Drizzle butter and parmesan cheese on top. Place the oysters in a pan.
7. Place the pan in the Big green egg cooker for another 5 minutes.
8. Serve warm.

Nutritional Information per Serving:

- Calories 351
- Total Fat 4 g
- Saturated Fat 6.3 g
- Cholesterol 360 mg
- Sodium 236 mg
- Total Carbs 19.1 g
- Sugar 0.3 g
- Fiber 0.1 g
- Protein 36 g

Smoked Pepper Tuna

Serving: 4
Prep Time: 10 minutes
Cooking Time: 10 minutes

Ingredients:

- 6 (4oz.) tuna steaks
- 3 tablespoons kosher salt
- 3 tablespoons light brown sugar
- 1/4 cup extra-virgin olive oil
- lemon pepper seasoning, to taste
- 1 teaspoon garlic powder
- 12 thin lemon slices

Method:

1. Preheat the Big green egg cooker to 350 degrees F without convEGGtor.
2. Rub the tuna steaks with salt and sugar from both the sides.
3. Cover the steaks and refrigerate for 4 hours or overnight.
4. Place the marinated steaks over a clean surface and wipe them out.
5. Brush each side with olive oil, garlic powder and lemon pepper seasoning.
6. Place the tuna steaks on the Big green egg cooker and top them with lemon slices.
7. Return the rack to the Big green egg cooker and cook for 10 minutes.
8. Transfer the tuna to the cutting board.
9. Let it rest for 5 minutes then serve with lemon wedges, corn salsa and avocado.

Nutritional Information per Serving:

- Calories 353
- Total Fat 7.5 g
- Saturated Fat 1.1 g
- Cholesterol 20 mg
- Sodium 297 mg
- Total Carbs 10.4 g
- Fiber 0.2 g
- Sugar 0.1 g
- Protein 13.1 g

Cured Salmon

Serving: 4
Prep Time: 10 minutes
Cooking Time: 20 minutes

Ingredients:

- 1 to 1-1/2-pound whole salmon fillet, skin and bones removed
- ½ cup unflavored vodka or tequila
- 1/4 cup kosher salt
- 1/4 cup brown sugar
- 2 tablespoon cracked black pepper
- 1 bunch of fresh dill, chopped
- 1/2 lemon, thinly sliced

Method:

1. Place and set the fish fillets in the baking dish and pour the alcohol over it.
2. Sprinkle sugar, salt and pepper over the salmon.
3. Place the lemon slices and dill on top.
4. Cover the dish with a plastic wrap and refrigerate for about 8 to 12 hours.
5. Preheat the Big green egg cooker to 350 degrees F without convEGGtor.
6. Discard the excess water from the marinated fish and rinse the filet under cold water.
7. Pat dry it with paper towels. Let them rest for 2 hours.
8. Grease the grill grates with olive oil and place the fish fillets on it.
9. Place the grilling grate in the Big green egg cooker and grill the fish for 10 minutes per side.
10. Serve warm.

Nutritional Information per Serving:

- Calories 321
- Total Fat 7.4 g
- Saturated Fat 4.6 g
- Cholesterol 105 mg
- Sodium 353 mg
- Total Carbs 19.4 g
- Sugar 6.5 g
- Fiber 2.7 g
- Protein 37.2 g

Lobster Tail Casserole

Serving: 6
Prep Time: 10 minutes
Cooking Time: 16 minutes

Ingredients

- 1 lb. salmon fillets, cut into 8 equal pieces
- 16 large sea scallops
- 16 large prawns, peeled and deveined
- 8 East Coast lobster tails split in half
- 1/3 cup butter
- 1/4 cup white wine
- 1/4 cup lemon juice
- 2 tbsp chopped fresh tarragon
- 2 medium garlic cloves, minced
- 1/2 tsp paprika
- 1/4 tsp ground cayenne pepper

Method:

1. Preheat the Big green egg cooker to 350 degrees F without convEGGtor.
2. Whisk butter with lemon juice, wine, garlic, tarragon, paprika, salt, and cayenne pepper in a small saucepan.
3. Stir cook this mixture over medium heat for 1 minute.
4. Toss the seafood in a baking dish and pour the butter mixture on top.
5. Bake in the preheated Green Egg Cooker for 15 minutes.
6. Serve warm.

Nutritional Information per Serving:

- Calories 248
- Total Fat 15.7 g
- Saturated Fat 2.7 g
- Cholesterol 75 mg
- Sodium 94 mg
- Total Carbs 31.4 g
- Fiber 0.4 g
- Sugar 3.1 g
- Protein 24.9 g

Baked Shrimp with Garlic Sauce

Prep Time: 10 minutes
Cooking Time: 10 minutes
Serving: 4

Ingredients

- 1 1/4 lbs large shrimp, peeled and deveined
- 1/4 cup butter
- 1 tbsp garlic, minced
- 2 tbsp fresh lemon juice
- Salt and black pepper, to taste
- 1/8 tsp red pepper flakes
- 2 tbsp fresh parsley, minced

Method:

1. Preheat the Big green egg cooker to 300 degrees F without convEGGtor.
2. Spread the shrimp in a baking dish.
3. Melt and heat butter in a pan and sauté garlic in it for 30 seconds.
4. Stir in lemon, then pour this mixture over the shrimp.
5. Drizzle salt, black pepper, and red pepper flakes over the shrimp.
6. Bake in the preheated Green Egg Cooker for 0 minutes.
7. Serve warm.

Nutritional Information per Serving:

- Calories 248
- Total Fat 13 g
- Saturated Fat 7 g
- Cholesterol 387 mg
- Sodium 353 mg
- Total Carbs 1 g
- Fiber 0.4 g
- Sugar 1 g
- Protein 29 g

Seafood Casserole

Prep Time: 10 minutes
Cooking Time: 20 minutes
Serving: 8

Ingredients

- 8 oz haddock, skinned and diced
- 1 lb scallops
- 1 lb large shrimp, peeled and deveined
- 3- 4 garlic cloves, minced
- 1/2 cup heavy cream
- 1/2 cup Swiss cheese, shredded
- 2 tbs Parmesan, grated
- Paprika, to taste
- Sea salt and black pepper, to taste

Method:

1. Preheat the Big green egg cooker to 375 degrees F without convEGGtor.
2. Toss shrimp, scallops, and haddock chunks in a baking dish greased with cooking spray.
3. Drizzle salt, black pepper, and minced garlic over the seafood mix.
4. Top this seafood with cream, Swiss cheese, paprika, and Parmesan cheese.
5. Bake in the preheated Green Egg Cooker for 20 minutes.
6. Serve warm.

Nutritional Information per Serving:

- Calories 457
- Total Fat 19.1 g
- Saturated Fat 11 g
- Cholesterol 262 mg
- Sodium 557 mg
- Total Carbs 18.9 g
- Sugar 1.2 g
- Fiber 1.7 g
- Protein 32.5 g

Garlic and Dill Seafood Bake

Prep Time: 10 minutes
Cooking Time: 30 minutes
Serving: 8

Ingredients

- 1 cup unsalted butter melted
- 3 tbsp fresh dill, chopped
- 2 tbsp garlic minced
- Salt, to taste
- Black pepper, to taste
- 24 oz baby red potato
- 4 fillets cod,
- 30 shrimp raw, peeled and deveined
- 8 lemon slices
- 4 corn ears, husked and halved

Method:

1. Preheat the Big green egg cooker to 450 degrees F without convEGGtor.
2. Cut the foil sheet into 8- 2 feet squares and place 4 pieces over a working surface.
3. Place the remaining pieces over these pieces to double them.
4. Spray each group of foil sheets with cooking oil to grease them.
5. Now melt butter in a glass bowl and add baby dill, black pepper, salt, and garlic.
6. Mix well and keep this dill butter aside.
7. Place each fish fillet over one square of greased foil then top it with 6 shrimp, 2 corn halves, ½ cup potatoes, and ¼ of the dill butter.
8. Finally, set 2 lemon slices on top of each fillet and wrap each foil sheet around the toppings.
9. Bake in the preheated Green Egg Cooker for 30 minutes.
10. Unwrap the baked fish and serve warm with the veggies.
11. Enjoy.

Nutritional Information per Serving:

- Calories 321
- Total Fat 7.4 g
- Saturated Fat 4.6 g
- Cholesterol 105 mg
- Sodium 353 mg
- Total Carbs 19.4 g
- Sugar 6.5 g
- Fiber 2.7 g
- Protein 37.2 g

Halibut Scallops Casserole

Prep Time: 10 minutes
Cooking Time: 12 minutes
Serving: 8

Ingredients

- 2 (4 oz.) halibut fillets, cubed
- 6 scallops
- 6 jumbo shrimp, peeled and deveined
- 1/3 cup dry white wine
- 2 tablespoons melted butter
- 1 tablespoon lemon juice
- 1/2 teaspoon Old Bay seasoning
- 1 teaspoon garlic, minced
- Salt and pepper to taste
- 1 tablespoon fresh parsley, chopped

Method:

1. Preheat the Big green egg cooker to 450 degrees F without convEGGtor.
2. Toss halibut chunks, shrimp, and scallops in a baking dish.
3. Whisk wine, lemon juice, and butter in a small bowl and pour over the seafood.
4. Drizzle seasoning, garlic, salt, and black pepper over the seafood mixture.
5. Bake in the preheated Green Egg Cooker for 12 minutes.
6. Garnish with parsley.
7. Serve warm.

Nutritional Information per Serving:

- Calories 392
- Total Fat 16.1 g
- Saturated Fat 2.3 g
- Cholesterol 231 mg
- Sodium 466 mg
- Total Carbs 3.9 g
- Sugar 0.6 g
- Fiber 0.9 g
- Protein 48 g

Chapter 8: Vegetables Recipes

BBQ Tofu Bowls

Serving: 4
Prep Time: 10 minutes
Cooking Time: 1 hour

Ingredients:

- 1 14-oz package extra-firm tofu, pressed for about 1 hour and cut into 1-inch cubes
- 1 tablespoon dry miso soup mix optional
- 8 oz. warm water for the marinade, also optional
- 1 cup BBQ sauce we like a Carolina style sauce
- 1 cup uncooked rice
- 2 cups of coconut water
- 2 cups pineapple cut into cubes and skewered
- 1 avocado thinly sliced
- 1 red bell pepper thinly sliced
- 1 carrot shredded or thinly sliced
- Cilantro for garnish

Method:

1. Drain and press the tofu under a heavy glass dish to squeeze out the liquid.
2. Place the tofu between two paper towels for 1 hour and soak excess water.

3. For the Tofu Marinade:
4. Mix 1 tablespoon miso soup with warm water in a Ziplock bag.
5. Slice the tofu into 1x1 inch cubes.
6. Add miso marinade to the tofu cubes.
7. Mix well and refrigerate for 30 minutes.

To Smoke the Tofu:
8. Preheat the Big green egg cooker to 350 degrees F without convEGGtor.
9. Remove the prepared tofu from the marinade and transfer to a bowl.
10. Add half cup BBQ sauce and mix well to coat.
11. Place the tofu cubes on the Big green egg cooker and cook for 1 hour.
12. Enjoy.

Nutritional Information per Serving:

- Calories 438
- Total Fat 4.8 g

- Saturated Fat 1.7 g
- Cholesterol 12 mg
- Sodium 520 mg
- Total Carbs 8.3 g

- Fiber 2.3 g
- Sugar 1.2 g
- Protein 2.1 g

Eggplant Ghanoush

Serving: 4
Prep Time: 10 minutes
Cooking Time: 1 hour

Ingredients:

- 2 medium eggplants, sliced
- 1 garlic clove, chopped
- 4 tablespoons tahini
- 3 tablespoons freshly squeezed lemon juice
- 2 teaspoons olive oil
- 1 teaspoon sea salt
- 1/2 teaspoon freshly ground pepper
- fresh flat-leaf parsley, chopped
- pita bread cut into triangles

Method:

1. Preheat the Big green egg cooker to 200 degrees F with convEGGtor.
2. Drizzle oil on the eggplants slices and place them in a foil pan.
3. Place the foil pan in the Big green egg cooker and cover the lid.
4. Let it smoke for 1 hour approximately until al dente.
5. Transfer the smoked eggplant to a food processor.
6. Add all the remaining ingredients and blend well until smooth.
7. Serve with your favorite bread.

Nutritional Information per Serving:

- Calories 294
- Total Fat 11.1 g
- Saturated Fat 5.8 g
- Cholesterol 610 mg
- Sodium 749 mg
- Total Carbs 49 g
- Fiber 0.2 g
- Sugar 0.2 g
- Protein 3.5 g

Fruit Salad

Serving: 4
Prep Time: 10 minutes
Cooking Time: 10 minutes

Ingredients:

- 1 pineapple, cored and cut into rounds
- 2 mangos, cut into 1-1/2-inch pieces
- 2 apples, cut into 1-1/2-inch rounds

Passion fruit sauce:

- 1/4 cup passion fruit extract
- 1/4 cup water

Mascarpone cream:

- 2 tablespoon sugar
- 1-pint heavy cream

- 1/4 cup large coconut flakes, toasted
- 1/4 cup sugar in the raw
- 1/2 cup coconut cream
- 1 tablespoon mint, chopped

- 1/2 cup sugar

- 1/4 cup mascarpone cheese

Method:

1. Preheat the Big green egg cooker to 375 degrees F without convEGGtor.
2. Spread the fruit in a sheet pan and top them with coconut cream and sugar.
3. Mix fruit puree, water and half cup sugar in a saucepan.
4. Bring the mixture to a boil then reduce the heat and let it simmer until it thickens.
5. Turn off the heat and refrigerate the mixture for 30 minutes.
6. Spread the fruits on the Big green egg cooker and grill for 3 to 5 minutes per side.
7. Remove the fruits and allow them to cool.
8. Whisk cream in a mixing bowl until it forms peaks.
9. Add mascarpone cheese and sugar. Whisk until well combined.
10. Toss in grilled fruits and mix well.
11. Stir in passion fruit sauce.
12. Mix well and serve.

Nutritional Information per Serving:

- Calories 341
- Total Fat 4 g
- Saturated Fat 0.5 g
- Cholesterol 69 mg
- Sodium 547 mg

- Total Carbs 36.4 g
- Fiber 1.2 g
- Sugar 1 g
- Protein 10.3 g

Seitan BBQ Ribs

Serving: 6
Prep Time: 10 minutes
Cooking Time: 20 minutes

Ingredients:

- 1 cup vital wheat gluten
- 2 tablespoons nutritional yeast
- 1 tablespoon smoked paprika
- 1 teaspoon onion powder
- 1 teaspoon garlic powder
- 2 tablespoons almond butter
- 1 tablespoon Soy sauce
- 3/4 cup water
- 1 teaspoon Worcestershire sauce
- 1 teaspoon apple cider vinegar

Method:

1. Preheat the Big green egg cooker to 370 degrees F without convEGGtor.
2. Mix the first five ingredients in a bowl.
3. Whisk water, almond butter, Worcestershire sauce, soy sauce, and apple cider vinegar in a separate bowl.
4. Pour this mixture into the dry mixture. Mix well.
5. Knead the dough for 2 minutes, then allow it to rest for 5 minutes.
6. Spread the dough into a rectangular shape.
7. Cut the dough into 10 equal pieces.
8. Place popsicles stick at the center of each piece and fold it in. Seal it through a pinch.
9. Arrange the wrapped Popsicle or seitan ribs in the Big green egg cooker for 20 minutes.
10. Brush the seitan ribs with BBQ sauce and grill for 4 minutes, then flip to coat the other side.
11. Serve warm.

Nutritional Information per Serving:

- Calories 378
- Total Fat 3.8 g
- Saturated Fat 0.7 g
- Cholesterol 2 mg
- Sodium 620 mg
- Total Carbs 13.3 g
- Fiber 2.4 g
- Sugar 1.2 g
- Protein 5.4 g

Spiced Cashews

Serving: 4
Prep Time: 10 minutes
Cooking Time: 20 minutes

Ingredients:

- 1 lb. cashews
- 3 tablespoons sambal Olek
- 1 tablespoon smoked simple syrup
- zest of 1 lemon
- 1/2 tablespoon fresh rosemary, chopped
- 1 teaspoon red pepper flakes
- 1/4 teaspoon cayenne powder

Method:

1. Preheat the Big green egg cooker to 350 degrees F with convEGGtor.
2. Mix all the ingredients with cashews in a bowl.
3. Spread the cashews in a sheet pan.
4. Place the pan in the Big green egg cooker and cook for 20 minutes.
5. Allow them to cool and serve.

Nutritional Information per Serving:

- Calories 304
- Total Fat 30.6 g
- Saturated Fat 13.1 g
- Cholesterol 131 mg
- Sodium 834 mg
- Total Carbs 21.4 g
- Fiber 0.2 g
- Sugar 0.3 g
- Protein 4.6 g

Pumpkin Soup

Serving: 4
Prep Time: 10 minutes
Cooking Time: 65 minutes

Ingredients:

- 1 pumpkin, cut in half
- 1 white onion, diced
- 1 garlic clove, minced
- ½ pint double cream
- Vegetable stock, as desired

Method:

1. Preheat the Big green egg cooker to 350 degrees F without convEGGtor.
2. Cut the washed pumpkin in half and remove the seeds.
3. Place the pumpkin halves in the Big green egg cooker with their skin downside.
4. Cook the pumpkin in the Big green egg cooker for 50 minutes.
5. Remove the pumpkin and allow it to cool.
6. Scoop out the pumpkin flesh and set it aside.
7. Heat oil in a suitable cooking pan, then add onion and garlic to sauté until soft.
8. Add pumpkin flesh and vegetable stock.
9. Bring the mixture to a boil, then reduce the heat to medium.
10. Let it simmer for 15 minutes.
11. Puree the mixture using a handheld blender.
12. Serve with pumpkin seeds on top.

Nutritional Information per Serving:

- Calories 338
- Total Fat 23.8 g
- Saturated Fat 0.7 g
- Cholesterol 22 mg
- Sodium 620 mg
- Total Carbs 58.3 g
- Fiber 2.4 g
- Sugar 1.2 g
- Protein 5.4 g

Smoked Green Beans

Serving: 2
Prep Time: 10 minutes
Cooking Time: 1 hour

Ingredients:

- 2 tablespoons Italian dressing
- 1 pound of green beans, trimmed
- Juice of 1/2 a lemon

Method:

1. Soak the trimmed bean in a bowl filled with water for 2 hours.
2. Drain and set the beans aside.
3. Preheat the Big green egg cooker to 300 degrees F without convEGGtor.
4. Prepare a rectangular pan out of aluminum foil and place the beans in it.
5. Mix the Italian dressing and uniformly drizzle it on the beans.
6. Place beans in the foil on the Big green egg cooker and cook for 1 hour.
7. Drizzle lemon juice over the beans and cover the beans with a foil.
8. Let them rest for 15 minutes at room temperature.
9. Serve.

Nutritional Information per Serving:

- Calories 100
- Total Fat 3.5 g
- Saturated Fat 0 g
- Cholesterol 7 mg
- Sodium 94 mg
- Total Carbs 15 g
- Fiber 1 g
- Sugar 1 g
- Protein 2 g

Smoked Aubergine

Serving: 4
Prep Time: 10 minutes
Cooking Time: 20 minutes

Ingredients:

- 2 whole aubergine, peeled and sliced lengthwise
- 2 spring onions, chopped
- 2 teaspoons sesame seeds
- 4 teaspoons miso paste
- 2 teaspoons soy sauce
- 1 teaspoon sesame oil
- 1 garlic clove
- 1-inch cube fresh ginger

Method:

1. Mix soy, sesame oil, miso, garlic clove, and ginger in a bowl.
2. Score the aubergine slices with the miso paste.
3. Let it sit for 30 minutes.
4. Preheat the Big green egg cooker to 350 degrees F without convEGGtor.
5. Grill the seasoned aubergine in a Big green egg cooker for 10 minutes per side.
6. Serve warm.

Nutritional Information per Serving:

- Calories 246
- Total Fat 14.8 g
- Saturated Fat 0.7 g
- Cholesterol 22 mg
- Sodium 220 mg
- Total Carbs 10.3 g
- Fiber 2.4 g
- Sugar 1.2 g
- Protein 12.4 g

Lemon Artichokes

Serving: 4
Prep Time: 10 minutes
Cooking Time: 30 minutes

Ingredients:

- 4 whole artichokes, trimmed
- 1/2 cup extra-virgin olive oil
- Juice of 1 lemon
- 4 minced garlic cloves
- Sea salt and cracked black pepper

Method:

1. Add water to a suitable pot and set a steaming basket in it.
2. Bring the water to a boil.
3. Meanwhile, clean and trim the artichokes. Slice them lengthwise.
4. Place the artichokes in the steam basket with their stem side down.
5. Reduce the heat and cover the pot.
6. Let it steam for 20 to 25 minutes.
7. Remove the artichokes and let them sit at room temperature.
8. Preheat the Big green egg cooker to 350 degrees F with convEGGtor.
9. Set the artichokes on aluminum foil packets.
10. Mix lemon juice, salt, pepper, olive oil in a bowl, and brush the mixture over the artichokes.
11. Set the artichokes in the Big green egg cooker.
12. Cover the lid and let it cook for 30 minutes.
13. Top with melted butter and serve.

Nutritional Information per Serving:

- Calories 118
- Total Fat 5.7 g
- Saturated Fat 2.7 g
- Cholesterol 75 mg
- Sodium 124 mg
- Total Carbs 7 g
- Fiber 0.1 g
- Sugar 0.3 g
- Protein 4.9 g

Balsamic Cabbage

Serving: 2
Prep Time: 10 minutes
Cooking Time: 1 1/2 hours

Ingredients:

- 1 small head of green cabbage
- 1 tablespoon balsamic vinegar
- 1/2 teaspoon sea salt
- 1/2 teaspoon black pepper
- 2 tablespoons butter
- 2 tablespoons olive oil
- Salt and black pepper to taste.

Method:

1. Preheat the Big green egg cooker to 350 degrees F with convEGGtor.
2. Remove the cabbage core such that it will get a cylindrical cavity inside about 1 inch wide and 3 inches deep.
3. Fill its cavity with salt, pepper, butter and vinegar.
4. Rub the outside of the cabbage with olive oil, salt and pepper.
5. Place the cabbage in the aluminium foil bag with its cut side up. Wrap it completely.
6. Arrange the foil bag in the Big green egg cooker and cover the lid.
7. Cook for 20 minutes in the cooker.
8. Slice into wedges and serve with applesauce.

Nutritional Information per Serving:

- Calories 191
- Total Fat 2.2 g
- Saturated Fat 2.4 g
- Cholesterol 10 mg
- Sodium 276 mg
- Total Carbs 7.7 g
- Fiber 0.9 g
- Sugar 1.4 g
- Protein 8.8 g

Buttered Corn Cob

Serving: 6
Prep Time: 10 minutes
Cooking Time: 35 minutes

Ingredients:

- 6 sweet corn cobs
- 2 tablespoons melted butter
- kosher salt and black pepper to taste

Method:

1. Soak the peeled corn in a bowl filled with water for 2 hours.
2. Preheat the Big green egg cooker to 300 degrees F without convEGGtor.
3. Drain the soaked corn knob and place them in the Big green egg cooker.
4. Cook for 30 minutes while rotating them after every 5 minutes.
5. Baste the knobs with butter while cooking.
6. Sprinkle salt and pepper on top.
7. Serve warm.

Nutritional Information per Serving:

- Calories 148
- Total Fat 22.4 g
- Saturated Fat 10.1 g
- Cholesterol 320 mg
- Sodium 350 mg
- Total Carbs 32.2 g
- Fiber 0.7 g
- Sugar 0.7 g
- Protein 4.3 g

Chapter 9: Desserts Recipes

Double layer Cake

Serving: 8
Prep Time: 15 minutes
Cooking Time: 25 minutes

Ingredients:

First Layer

- 3 tablespoons all-purpose flour
- 1/4 cup sugar, powdered
- 1 teaspoon baking powder
- 1 tablespoon gelatine
- 8 tablespoons butter
- 1/2 teaspoon vanilla essence
- 2 large eggs

Second Layer

- 8 tablespoons butter
- 8 oz. cream cheese
- 1/2 teaspoon vanilla essence
- Liquid stevia, to taste
- 2 large eggs

Method:

1. At 350 degrees F, preheat your Green Egg Cooker with a convEGGtor.
2. Take an 8-inch springform pan and butter it to grease well.

First layer

3. Beat vanilla and butter in all the eggs in a mixer.
4. Stir in gelatine, baking powder, flour, and gelatine.
5. Mix well until everything is well incorporated. Set this mixture aside.

Second Layer

6. Beat the butter with cream cheese separately in an electric mixer.
7. Add stevia and vanilla essence for flavor. Then whisk in eggs.
8. Beat everything until the mixture is smooth.

Assembly

9. First, spread the first layer in the greased baking pan.
10. Then top this layer with batter from the second layer evenly.
11. Bake the cake for 25 minutes in the Green Egg Cooker.

12. Once done, remove the cake from the cooker and allow it to cool on a wire rack,
13. Refrigerate for 2 hours in a wrapped plastic sheet.
14. Slice and serve.

Nutritional Information per Serving:

- Calories 336
- Total Fat 34.5 g
- Saturated Fat 21.4 g
- Cholesterol 139 mg
- Sodium 267 mg
- Total Carbs 9.1 g
- Sugar 0.2 g
- Fiber 1.1 g
- Protein 5.1 g

Citrus Cream Cake

Serving: 4
Prep Time: 15 minutes
Cooking Time: 60 minutes

Ingredients:

Cake

- ¾ teaspoons vanilla essence
- 4 whole eggs
- ¼ cup butter, unsalted softened
- 1 ¼ cups all-purpose flour
- 3/4 cup sugar

- ¼ teaspoon lemon essence
- ¼ teaspoon salt
- 4 ounces cream cheese
- ¾ teaspoons baking powder

Cream Frosting

- 1/8 cup sugar
- 1 ½ tablespoon heavy whipping cream

- ¼ teaspoon vanilla essence

Method:

1. At 350 degrees F, preheat your Green Egg Cooker with a convEGGtor.
2. Meanwhile, beat butter with sugar and cream cheese in a suitable bowl.
3. Stir in eggs, lemon essence, and vanilla beat well.
4. Whisk in baking powder, salt, and all-purpose flour.
5. Once the batter is combined well, transfer it to a greased baking pan.
6. Bake the cake in the Green Egg Cooker for 60 minutes.
7. Beat all the ingredients for the frosting in a suitable bowl.
8. Once done, remove the cake from the pan and place it over the wire rack.
9. Let it cool for 10 mins then spread the cream frosting on its top.
10. Refrigerate the cake for 30 minutes or more.
11. Slice and serve to enjoy.

Nutritional Information per Serving:

- Calories 255
- Total Fat 23.4 g
- Saturated Fat 11.7 g
- Cholesterol 135 mg
- Sodium 112 mg

- Total Carbs 2.5 g
- Sugar 12.5 g
- Fiber 1 g
- Protein 7.9 g

Zesty Lemon Cake

Serving: 8
Prep Time: 15 minutes
Cooking Time: 45 minutes

Ingredients:

Cake

- 1/2 cup all-purpose flour
- 5 eggs
- 1/4 cup Sugar
- 1/2 cup butter, melted
- Juice from 1/2 lemon
- 1/2 teaspoon lemon zest
- 1/2 teaspoon xanthan gum
- 1/2 teaspoon salt

Icing

- 1 cup cream cheese
- 3 tablespoons sugar
- 1 teaspoon vanilla essence
- ½ teaspoon lemon zest

Method:

1. At 335 degrees F, preheat your Green Egg Cooker with a convEGGtor.
2. Whisk and beat egg whites using an electric mixer until it forms stiff peaks.
3. Put everything else in another bowl and mix them well.
4. Once well-combined, fold in egg white foam and whisk it gently.
5. Use a spatula to transfer the batter to a 9x5 inch loaf pan, greased with oil.
6. Bake the foamy batter in the Green Egg Cooker for 45 minutes.
7. Meanwhile, prepare the topping by beating icing ingredients in the electric mixer.
8. Place the baked cake on the wire rack and let it cool for 10 minutes.
9. Spread the cream cheese icing over the cake and spread it evenly.
10. Refrigerate for 30 minutes or more.
11. Garnish as desired.
12. Slice and enjoy after a meal.

Nutritional Information per Serving:

- Calories 251
- Total Fat 24.5 g
- Saturated Fat 14.7 g
- Cholesterol 165 mg
- Sodium 142 mg
- Total Carbs 4.3 g
- Sugar 0.5 g
- Fiber 1 g
- Protein 5.9 g

Cream Cake

Serving: 8
Prep Time: 15 minutes
Cooking Time: 60 minutes

Ingredients:

Cream Cheese Icing:

- 8 oz. cream cheese softened
- 1/2 cup butter softened
- 1/2 cup powdered Sugar
- 1 teaspoon vanilla essence optional
- 2 tablespoons heavy cream

Carrot Cake Layers:

- 5 eggs large
- 3/4 cup sugar
- 2 teaspoons vanilla essence
- 14 tablespoons butter melted
- 1/4 teaspoon unsweetened coconut, shredded
- 1/4 teaspoon salt
- 1/2 cup almond flour
- 1 3/4 cup all-purpose flour
- 2 teaspoons baking powder
- 1 1/2 teaspoon cinnamon, ground
- 1 1/4 cup shredded carrots

Method:

1. Beat all the ingredients for the icing in an electric mixer until foamy. Set it aside.

For carrot cake layers:

2. At 350 degrees F, preheat your Green Egg Cooker with a convEGGtor.
3. Layer two 8-inch baking pan with parchment paper.
4. Grease the baking pans and set them aside.
5. Beat eggs with sugar in an electric mixer for 5 minutes until foamy.
6. Mix all-purpose flour with salt, almond flour, baking powder, and cinnamon.
7. Transfer this mixture to the egg batter and mix well until smooth.
8. Fold in coconut, butter, melted, and carrots. Stir well.
9. Divide the cake batter into two pans and bake each for 30 minutes in the Green Egg Cooker.
10. Set them to cool for about 15 minutes once baked.

To Assemble:

11. Top 1 cake with half of the icing mixture.
12. Place another cake on top of it.

13. Spread the remaining icing on the top of the upper layer.
14. Garnish as desired.
15. Slice and serve.

Nutritional Information per Serving:

- Calories 307
- Total Fat 29 g
- Saturated Fat 14g
- Cholesterol 111 mg
- Sodium 122 mg
- Total Carbs 7 g
- Sugar 1 g
- Fiber 3 g
- Protein 6 g

Buttery Chocolate Cake

Serving: 6
Prep Time: 15 minutes
Cooking Time: 46 minutes

Ingredients:

- 7 oz. sugar-free dark chocolate
- 3.5 oz. butter
- 3.4 oz. cream
- 4 egg whites
- 4 egg yolks
- sugar to taste

Method:

1. At 325 degrees F, preheat your Green Egg Cooker with a convEGGtor.
2. Take an 8-inch baking pan and rub some butter in it to grease it.
3. Melt the remaining butter with chocolate in the microwave, then mix well.
4. Once melted, add cream and sugar to the chocolate mixture.
5. Beat in egg yolks and beat until it is well incorporated.
6. Whisk egg white within another mixing bowl until it turns foamy.
7. Fold the white egg foam into the creamy butter mixture.
8. Use a spatula to transfer the batter to the prepared baking pan.
9. Bake it in the Green Egg Cooker for 45 minutes.
10. Remove the cake from the pan and place it over the wire rack.
11. Let it cool for 5 mins then refrigerate it for 4 hours packed in a plastic sheet.
12. Slice and serve the cake.

Nutritional Information per Serving:

- Calories 173
- Total Fat 16.2 g
- Saturated Fat 9.8 g
- Cholesterol 100 mg
- Sodium 42 mg
- Total Carbs 9.4 g
- Sugar 0.2 g
- Fibre1 g
- Protein 3.3 g

Chunky Carrot Cake

Serving: 8
Prep Time: 15 minutes
Cooking Time: 60 minutes

Ingredients:

- 3/4 cup sugar
- 3/4 cup butter
- 1 teaspoon vanilla essence
- 1/2 teaspoon pineapple extract
- 4 large egg
- 2 1/2 cup all-purpose flour
- 2 teaspoons gluten-free baking powder
- 2 teaspoons cinnamon
- 1/2 teaspoon sea salt
- 2 1/2 cup carrots, grated
- 1 cup pecans, chopped
- Pecans, to garnish

Method:

1. At 350 degrees F, preheat your Green Egg Cooker with a convEGGtor.
2. Grease the base of two 9-inch baking dishes and layer it with parchment paper.
3. Beat sugar in cream in a suitable bowl.
4. Stir in vanilla essence and pineapple extract.
5. While beating this mixture, start adding eggs one by one.
6. Add cinnamon, salt, baking powder, and flour to this mixture.
7. Whisk well to combine.
8. Fold in 1 cup chopped pecans and carrots.
9. Divide the entire batter into the two pans.
10. Bake each for 30 minutes in the Green Egg Cooker.
11. Remove both the cakes from the pans and let them cool for 10 minutes on wire racks.
12. Use the remaining pecans to garnish it.
13. Slice and serve.

Nutritional Information per Serving:

- Calories 359
- Total Fat 34 g
- Saturated Fat 10.3 g
- Cholesterol 112 mg
- Sodium 92 mg
- Total Carbs 8.5 g
- Sugar 2 g
- Fiber 1.3 g
- Protein 7.5 g

Pecan Cake

Serving: 8
Prep Time: 15 minutes
Cooking Time: 1 hour 30 minutes

Ingredients:

Cake

- 1/2 cup butter softened
- 1 cup Sugar
- 4 large eggs, separated
- 1/2 cup heavy cream
- 1 teaspoon vanilla essence
- 1 1/2 cups all-purpose flour
- 1/2 cup coconut, shredded
- 1/2 cup pecans, chopped
- 1/4 cup almond flour
- 2 teaspoons baking powder
- 1/2 teaspoon salt
- 1/4 teaspoon tartar cream

Frosting

- 8 ounces cream cheese softened
- 1/2 cup heavy whipping cream
- 1/2 cup butter softened
- 1 cup powdered Sugar
- 1 teaspoon vanilla essence

Garnish

- 2 tablespoons coconut, shredded and toasted
- 2 tablespoons pecans, chopped and toasted

Method:

Cake

1. At 325 degrees F, preheat your Green Egg Cooker with a convEGGtor.
2. Take two 8 inches baking pan and grease them with butter.
3. Beat egg yolks with cream, sugar, butter, and vanilla in a mixed.
4. Combine all the flours, chopped pecans, salt, baking powder, and coconut shred.
5. Add this mixture to the egg yolk batter and mix well.
6. Beat egg whites separately in a mixer until foamy.
7. Fold this foamy mixture into the flour batter.
8. Now divide the batter into the baking pans.
9. Bake each for 45 minutes in the preheated Green Egg Cooker.
10. Remove each cake from their baking pan and let them cool on the wire rack.

Frosting

11. Combine and whisk all ingredients for frosting in a mixer until frothy.
12. Keep it aside.

To Assemble

13. First, place one cake on a plate.
14. Spread a layer of half of the frosting over its top evenly.
15. Place the second cake over it and cover it with the remaining frosting.
16. Garnish it with coconut shred and pecans.
17. Chill the baked cake for 30 minutes in the refrigerator.
18. Slice and serve.

Nutritional Information per Serving:

- Calories 267
- Total Fat 44.5 g
- Saturated Fat 17.4 g
- Cholesterol 153 mg
- Sodium 217 mg
- Total Carbs 8.4 g
- Sugar 2.3 g
- Fiber 1.3 g
- Protein 3.1 g

Strawberry Vanilla Tart

Serving: 8
Prep Time: 15 minutes
Cooking Time: 10 minutes

Ingredients:

Crust:

- 1/2 cup coconut oil
- 3/4 cup 2 tablespoons all-purpose flour
- 2 eggs
- 1 teaspoon vanilla essence
- 1 teaspoon powdered sugar

Cream Filling:

- 1 cup mascarpone
- 2 eggs separated
- 1 teaspoon vanilla essence
- 1-2 tablespoons powdered sugar
- 1 cup strawberries

Method:

Crust:

1. At 350 degrees F, preheat your Green Egg Cooker with a convEGGtor.
2. Beat eggs in a suitable bowl, then add the rest of the ingredients.
3. Spread this dough in between two sheets of parchment paper.
4. Place this dough sheet in a greased pan and pierce holes in it using a fork.
5. Bake this crust for 10 minutes in the Green Egg Cooker.

Cream Filling:

6. Beat the egg whites in an electric mixer until frothy.
7. Stir in mascarpone cream, egg yolks, sugar, and vanilla and beat for 2 minutes.
8. Spread this filling in the baked crust evenly.
9. Top the filling with the sugar and strawberries.
10. Place the pie in the refrigerator for 30 minutes.
11. Slice and serve.

Nutritional Information per Serving:

- Calories 236
- Total Fat 21.5 g
- Saturated Fat 15.2 g
- Cholesterol 54 mg
- Sodium 21 mg
- Total Carbs 7.6 g
- Sugar 1.4 g
- Fiber 3.8 g
- Protein 4.3 g

Allspice Almond Cake

Serving: 8
Prep Time: 15 minutes
Cooking Time: 25 minutes

Ingredients:

For the cake:

- 1/2 cup sugar
- 5 tablespoons butter softened
- 4 large eggs
- 2 tablespoons unsweetened almond milk
- 1 teaspoon vanilla

- 1 1/2 cups all-purpose flour
- 2 tablespoons bread flour
- 1 tablespoon baking powder
- 1 1/2 teaspoon cinnamon, ground
- 1/4 teaspoon ground allspice
- 1/2 cup almonds

Cream Cheese Frosting:

- 4 oz. cream cheese softened
- 2 tablespoons butter softened
- 1 teaspoon vanilla

- 1 tablespoon heavy cream
- 1/4 cup confectioners' sugar

Method:

1. At 350 degrees F, preheat your Green Egg Cooker with a convEGGtor.
2. Take a 9-inch pan and line it with parchment paper.
3. Beat sugar in butter in a suitable bowl until foamy.
4. Whisk in vanilla, eggs, and milk.
5. Beat well, then stir in spices, all-purpose flour, bread flour, and baking powder.
6. Now add the almond to this batter and mix gently.
7. Pour the almond batter into the baking pan and spread it evenly.
8. Bake it for 25 minutes in the Green Egg Cooker.
9. Meanwhile, beat frosting ingredients in a bowl until creamy.
10. Once the cake is made, remove it from the pan and place it over a wire rack.
11. After ten minutes, spread the frosting over the cake evenly.
12. Refrigerate for 30 minutes or more.
13. Slice and serve.

Nutritional Information per Serving:

- Calories 331
- Total Fat 38.5 g

- Saturated Fat 19.2 g
- Cholesterol 141 mg

- Sodium 283 mg
- Total Carbs 9.2 g
- Sugar 3 g
- Fiber 1 g
- Protein 2.1 g

Blackberry Lemon Tart

Serving: 8
Prep Time: 15 minutes
Cooking Time: 15 minutes

Ingredients:

- 1 cup lemon curd
- 1 cup blackberries

Pie Crust

- 1.5 cup all-purpose flour
- 1/2 cup almond flour
- 4 tablespoons sugar, powdered

- 1 tablespoon sliced almonds
- 2 9" tart molds with loose bottoms

- 2 eggs
- 4 tablespoons cold butter, unsalted

Method:

1. At 350 degrees F, preheat your Green Egg Cooker with a convEGGtor.
2. Prepare the dough by mixing everything for the pie crust.
3. Divide the dough into two equal-sized balls.
4. Take two tart molds and layer it with oil and parchment paper.
5. Spread one dough ball into each pan and press it evenly.
6. Make a few holes into each dough layer using a fork.
7. Bake the tart crusts for 15 mins in the Green Egg Cooker.
8. Place the tart pans on a wire pan to cool the crust at room temperature.
9. Fill both the crusts with lemon curd equally.
10. Top it with berries, sugar, and almond slices.
11. Serve and enjoy.

Nutritional Information per Serving:

- Calories 321
- Total Fat 12.9 g
- Saturated Fat 5.1 g
- Cholesterol 17 mg
- Sodium 28 mg

- Total Carbs 8.1 g
- Sugar 1.8 g
- Fiber 0.4 g
- Protein 5.4 g

Conclusion

Cooking on the Big Green Egg showcases this vital piece of outdoor cooking equipment and offers instructions and recipes for everything you'd ever want to cook in it. The essential cookbook for your Big Green Egg smoker and grill, to smoke beef, pork, ham, lamb, fish and seafood, poultry, veggies, and game. Includes clear instructions and step-by-step directions for every recipe.

Get your springtime grilling ideas going with Big Green Egg Cookbook 2021-2020, the complete guide to charcoal smoking, grilling and roasting. We have collected more than 800-Day Flavorful Succulent Barbecue Recipes that will truly make you and your guests happy and satisfied.

What are you waiting for? Buy it now! And enjoy the most delicious meals.

CPSIA information can be obtained
at www.ICGtesting.com
Printed in the USA
LVHW061520291121
704740LV00003B/241